Questioning Psychological Health and Well-Being

Endowed by

Tom Watson Brown

and

The Watson-Brown Foundation, Inc.

Questioning Psychological Health and Well-Being

Historical and Contemporary Dialogues between Theologians and Psychologists

Britt-Mari Sykes

Mercer University Press
Macon, Georgia

MUP/P399

1400 Coleman Avenue
Macon, Georgia 31207

First Edition.

Books published by Mercer University Press are printed on acid free paper that meets the requirements of American National Standard for Information Sciences—Permanence of Paper for Printed Library Materials.

Mercer University Press is a member of Green Press initiative (greenpressinitiative.org), a nonprofit organization working to help publishers and printers increase their use of recycled paper and decrease their use of fiber derived from endangered forests. This book is printed on recycled paper.

Library of Congress Cataloging-in-Publication Data is available from the LOC

ISBN 13: 978-0-88146-171-8

Contents

1. Introduction 1

2. Paul Tillich and the New York Psychology Group, 1941-1945 11

3. The Meaning of My Existence and the Responsibility for Our Existence: Viktor E. Frankl's Existential Challenge to Psychology 45

4. Hans Hofman and the Harvard Project on Religion and Mental Health: 1956 to 1961 80

5. Contemporary Issues: The Challenge of Critical Psychology 101

6. "In the Midst of This World I Discover Myself Unmistakably": Alfried Längle's Theory of Existential Analysis 127

7. Concluding Remarks 154

Bibliography 157

Index 169

To Marjorie, Susan, and Hannah—

Grandmother, Mother, and Daughter

Acknowledgements

I am indebted to Dr. Alfried Längle of Vienna, Austria. I first met Dr. Längle in summer 2002 when he gave the keynote address to a conference on meaning in Vancouver, British Columbia. His address introduced the audience to his psychological theory and therapy of existential analysis and was, for me, the discovery of a deeply authentic and meaningful psychological theory that corresponded with my thoughts on development, health, and individual potential. Existential analysis offered a framework for exploring and analyzing these issues, and Dr. Längle's theory, friendship, and working collaborations have had a tremendous influence on my life.

This book is about dialogue and exploring not only the shape and meaning of psychological health and development, but also our unique capacity as human beings to come together, to think and work creatively on the topic of what makes us tick. I would like to thank several academic friends and colleagues who embody this creative search and with whom I have shared so many deeply enriching conversations: Terry D. Cooper, Matthew Lon Weaver, and Peter LeCour. In particular, I would like to acknowledge and thank Terry D. Cooper for his support, wonderful sense of humor, and invitations to share his classrooms in St. Louis with me so that I could do what I love—to share these ideas, stories, and theories with students.

I would also like to thank Marc Jolley, Marsha Luttrell, and Kevin Manus-Pennings of Mercer University Press for their interest in and support of this project.

Finally, I would like to thank my family: husband Kimball and daughter Hannah. What a rich life we share together! Thank you for keeping me so preoccupied with you!

1

Introduction

> Mankind has always tried to decipher the puzzling fragments of life. That attempt is not just a matter for the philosophers or priests or prophets or wise men in all periods of history. It is a matter for everyone. For every man is a fragment himself. He is a riddle to himself; and the individual life of everyone else is an enigma to him, dark, puzzling, embarrassing, exciting, and torturing. Our very being is a continuous asking for the *meaning* of our being, a continuous attempt to decipher the enigma of our world and our heart.[1]

We begin this book with a quotation from theologian Paul Tillich that I believe encapsulates the search, the questioning, and, ultimately, the ambiguity that confronts us when we attempt to know who we are as human beings. This quotation highlights the search and dialogue we need to engage in continuously and creatively. In this spirit, this book examines our ideas about psychological health, well-being, and development through an interdisciplinary lens of psychology and theology. Analyzing the meaning of psychological health and well-being reveals how inherently ambiguous and fluid these concepts are and inevitably invites existential, philosophical, religious, and ethical questions about who we are and the meaning and purpose of our existence. This kind of analysis raises the issue of care, both for ourselves and others, and thus points to a responsibility we all share in our collective well-being, regardless of whether we are in the fields of psychology or theology.

I see this book as a series of essays that highlight some of the ideas, questions, and debates that emerged mid-twentieth century in interdisciplinary dialogue between theologians and psychologists while simultaneously illustrating how many of these ideas remain salient today, particularly for those within the discipline of psychology who are

---

[1] Paul Tillich, "Knowledge Through Love" in *The Shaking of the Foundations* (New York: Charles Scribner's Sons, 1948) 111.

attempting to enlarge our conceptualizations of health and well-being. I have chosen to focus on three specific historical illustrations in which theologians and psychologists came together during the mid-twentieth century in the United States in order to discuss psychology's place in our culture as well as its growing influence on our images of selfhood and our definitions of health and well-being. These illustrations are the New York Psychology Group from 1941 to 1945 (chapter 2), Viktor Frankl's first lecture series at Harvard Divinity School in 1957 (chapter 3), and the Harvard Project on Religion and Mental Health (chapter 4). I chose to highlight these particular moments because the contributions and commitment of theologians Paul Tillich and Hans Hofmann and psychoanalyst Viktor Frankl to interdisciplinary dialogue during the mid-twentieth century brought them together intellectually and, in some cases, in actual working collaborations at various points. Paul Tillich's and Viktor Frankl's interest in these subjects had a lasting influence on their writings and perspectives on human nature.

The theologians and psychologists who joined what has been loosely described as the mental health movement in the mid-twentieth century were motivated by several factors. These included the rapid social and political changes occurring worldwide, the growing influence and expansion of the discipline of psychology, and the perceived decline in religious belief and participation. On the broader issue of human nature, they saw the dangers inherent in a purely scientific approach to the study of humankind versus seeing human beings as complex, varied, and ultimately unknowable. These interdisciplinary discussions yielded, therefore, some of the following large but compelling questions. What was the meaning of psychological health? What were the constituents of a productive, healthy, and fulfilling existence? How is psychological health linked to responsibility, love, care of self and others, and awareness of and engagement in the world?

What continues to fascinate me is that many of the ideas and debates prominent during the mid-twentieth century foreshadow our current reflections and provide a strong contextual foundation for much of contemporary debate. Postmodern theories such as critical psychology, although raising many similar questions, rarely utilize historical material, especially religious or theological contributions. While critical psychology mounts an important debate for the discipline of psychology, it seems unaware of a rich historical foundation and perspective for many of its enquiries. In chapter 4, I give a brief overview of this postmodern approach to psychological care and conclude with an interdisciplinary response drawing on two voices from the past, Viktor Frankl's and Paul Tillich's.

The resurgence in interdisciplinary or integrative approaches to psychology and mental health that take seriously the role of religion and spirituality in human expression and behavior once again marks a great change in how we see and interpret our capabilities as human beings. Purely scientific approaches to psychological health are increasingly seen as inadequate when we take seriously the deepest questions, the questions of ultimate concern, questions about the meaning of our very being, that patients and clients frequently express. Further, how can psychology, as science, broach issues of compassion, responsibility, being good to those around us, being good to thc world around us, our desire to dialogue with others, our desire to connect with others, and our capacity to search for meaning and fulfillment? We may debate whether these issues are psychological inquiries and how they might be tied to health and well-being, but they are expressions of what Viktor Frankl would describe as our very humanness and Alfried Längle would describe as fundamental existence questions. Further, these broad philosophical and ethical issues find expression at the individual level in our behaviors, feelings, attitudes, choices, and decisions. And they are, in many cases, the substance of therapeutic dialogue. The question that remains a constant challenge is how does psychology, indeed, how do therapists, approach these more philosophical and ethical inquiries? To this end, I offer an illustration in chapter 6 that focuses on Alfried Längle's contemporary theory of existential psychotherapy and conclude with an interdisciplinary dialogue between existential analysis and Paul Tillich's theories. Existential analysis is one therapeutic model that attempts to bridge practical therapeutic help with more philosophical questions about the meaning of psychological health, particularly the ambiguity, complexity, and depth of what it is to be human. Again, it is my contention that the themes about human nature, the meaning of health, and the links between individual and cultural development that emerged in the mid-twentieth century through interdisciplinary dialogue and collaboration between theologians and psychologists remain not only salient but have reemerged in contemporary debate and theory and continue to challenge and expand our visions of health and well-being.

The Emergence of a Religion and Mental Health Dialogue

During the mid-twentieth century in the United States, many dialogues occurred between theologians and psychologists. These interdisciplinary collaborations sought to challenge the social sciences that, they claimed, had contributed to advancing the Western ideology of individualism while omitting the value and dignity of individual life and the relational essence of being human. These critics argued that the ambiguity and precariousness of being human was unacknowledged, particularly by psychological scientism.

The various dialogues that took place in the mid-twentieth century focused on a relational and ethical view of individual development. The value and dignity of the individual was seen simultaneously as a reflection or microcosm of the larger world. Inextricably linked and grounded in both historical and present-day cultural, economic, political, and religious contexts, the individual was seen as both a receptive agent of these contexts and a responsive agent capable and ethically drawn to contributing to and shaping these same landscapes. Seeing the individual as a relational being exposed the fluidity in concepts such as self and world. This, in turn, revealed the ambiguity and near impossibility of truly capturing the essence of human experience. That ambiguity, however, was not seen as negative. Rather, acknowledging the ambiguous nature of human existence was seen as providing a positive impetus for continuous creative questions and pursuits about our human potential. Human nature, experience, and potential were seen as directional and continuous. As such, these dialogues differed quite dramatically from the closed theoretical systems favored by the social and pure sciences.

Throughout this book, the substantial issue of what constitutes health, specifically mental health, emerges continuously. Within this larger perspective, I look at several factors connecting religion and mental health. One factor is the dramatic rise of psychiatry and psychoanalysis in Western culture and the subsequent increase in the acceptance of these fields and their perspectives by the general public. Another factor is the Second World War, which created a growing public awareness of health care issues in light of the severe psychiatric disorders experienced by some returned soldiers.[2] This problem, in turn, led many, in what Allison Stokes calls the "new liberal intelligensia [*sic*]"[3] in the United States, to begin questioning a growing dependence on social scientific paradigms to analyze and prescribe ways to achieve "a normal healthy life." In terms of interdisciplinary dialogue, this new liberal intelligentsia, made up, among others, of social scientists and liberal Protestant theologians (many of whom had come from war-torn Europe), shared an overarching ethical concern to preserve humanity and Western civilization. That common concern brought the traditionally separate cultural discourses of theology and psychology together in dialogue.

Seward Hiltner, a prominent figure in pastoral counseling in the United States and a member of the New York Psychology Group from 1941 to 1945, wrote frequently on the relationship and dialogue between psychology and religion. Like so many of his colleagues, Hiltner linked general themes of human freedom and transformation to questions of what constituted individual mental health. In 1943, he commented on the peculiarity of using "normal" as a benchmark in defining mental health. The meaning of normal was itself problematic. He stated, "Science frequently flounders when dealing with the 'normal,' unless it be dealing with the average. Such definitions of health as 'efficient and happy living' do not seem to help us much."[4] Was health perceived as the absence of something or was it something more? Could the definition of mental health be expanded, and if it were to be expanded, what would it cover? In the mid-twentieth century, Hiltner wondered whether definitions of health should be expanded to include larger ethical and social issues or whether that would complicate matters even further. As we will see in chapter 2, members of the New York Psychology Group, both theologians and psychologists alike, spoke passionately about expanding the definition of psychological health and did this with a tone of urgent social, ethical, humanitarian, and political appeal.

---

[2] Eva Moskowitz offers a very good history of the rise of psychiatric disorders in the United States following WWII. Eva S. Moskowitz, *In Therapy We Trust: America's Obsession with Self-Fulfillment* (Baltimore MD: John Hopkins University Press, 2001).

[3] Allison Stokes, *Ministry After Freud* (New York: Pilgrim Press, 1985) n.p.

[4] Seward Hiltner, *Religion and Health* (New York: Macmillan Company, 1943) 82.

The existential psychologist Rollo May, also a member of the New York Psychology Group, offered an illuminating analysis of this period and the subsequent emergence of "American" existential psychotherapies in the 1960s. In an article in the 1961–1962 issue of the *Journal of Religion and Health*, May outlined the "cultural conditions" that had led to the development of existential psychology in Europe. He wrote:

> Called forth by the experience of tragedy, especially in Europe between the two wars, by the confronting of the contradictions in modern rationalism; and by the conviction that our usual approaches to the science of [man] in psychology and psychiatry did not touch the nature of [man] or the deepest well-springs of [his] behavior and experience...our European colleagues believed, too, that our sciences of [man] played into the very tendencies in the modern industrial developments to sap the individual's sense of worth and responsibility.[5]

May was also aware of the growing experiences of emptiness and meaninglessness that clients were expressing to therapists in a time of rapid technological, scientific, and cultural change during the postwar period. He wondered whether psychology's reliance on science and the development of psychological technique to adjust a person to "good health" did not, in fact, support a particular social ethic and require patients to conform to an implicit value system based on modern culture and its vision of humankind. It was from such concerns that the existential psychologies emerged with their focus on the value and dignity of each individual inextricably linked to the social world. "In my judgment," May wrote, "the existential approach is the achieving of individuality not by by-passing or avoiding the conflictual realities of the world in which we find ourselves—which for us happens to be Western culture—but by confronting and meeting these realities directly to achieve individuality and meaningful interpersonal relations."[6] The problem May spotted was that psychology, by internalizing a technological and scientific vision or philosophy of humankind, was well on its way to simplifying and reducing human behavior and action. May wrote, "The endeavor to understand phenomena by isolating out the simpler aspects of the behavior and making

---

[5] Rollo May, "Existential Psychiatry," *Journal of Religion and Health*, 1 (October 1961–1962) 32.

[6] Ibid., 35.

abstractions of them, such as drive and force, is useful in some aspects of science, but is not adequate for a science of [man] that will help us understand human anxiety, despair and other problems that beset the human psyche."[7]

The Harvard Project on Religion and Mental Health provides another rich historical illustration of theologians and psychologists coming together to question the aim, purpose, and applicability of psychological theory. The Harvard project addressed the contemporary minister's role in light of the powerful influence of psychology on mid-century culture and the effect that influence had on the issues and problems parishioners brought to their minister's attention. Again, in order to discuss and analyze these issues, interdisciplinary collaboration was seen as the most fruitful approach. The Harvard project, therefore, engaged the participation of Harvard professors from the departments of theology, psychology, and sociology in this endeavor. At the same time, the interdisciplinary nature of the project also elicited reflective analysis on religion itself and its place and relevance in contemporary society. Hofmann wrote,

> The question is whether a human being, troubled by our time and [his] place in it, can be healthy and productive merely by submitting to the tenets and rituals which [his] religion prescribes for [him]. Is it possible that religion should play a different role? Religion itself may prove to be one area of life—perhaps the one that offers the most profound possibilities of all—where the struggle with personal turmoil can provide the means to a radical renewal of our society and culture.[8]

We could substitute psychology for religion in this quotation of Hofmann's and ask whether a human being can be healthy and productive merely by submitting to the tenets and rituals which psychology prescribes for him or her? The argument throughout this book is that mental health and well-being are in fact contingent upon dialogue, contingent upon the simultaneous valuing of the individual and a valuing of the interrelational reality of human life. Context, relationship, and dialogue shift psychology's emphasis on the known "self" to the unknown, the ambiguous, and the fragments of human potential waiting to be

---

[7] Ibid., 37.

[8] Hans Hofmann, *Religion and Mental Health: A Casebook with Commentary and an Essay on Pertinent Literature* (New York: Harper and Brothers, 1961) xiv.

continuously deciphered. Hofmann's "radical renewal of our society and culture," a wish echoed by voices within contemporary critical psychology, can only happen through dialogue.

A common sentiment that ran throughout these groups' discussions was that human nature could not be adequately approached and studied from strictly scientific, religious, or cultural perspectives. Each one on its own ran the risk of offering a closed system or at the least a narrow perspective of humankind. What weaves throughout these interdisciplinary discussions is the possibility for change and transformation. This included both individuals and societies. Addressing individual health and well-being, therefore, also meant addressing our response and commitment to caring for our fellow human beings. Individuals were seen as relational beings, and that relational nature, in turn, precluded a foundation of ethical relating, or at least the possibility and choice of ethical relating.

Numerous publications also emerged through the late 1940s and into the early 1960s that addressed the relationship between psychology and religion, specifically issues of spirituality and mental health. These writings expressed a very similar thesis: Twentieth century Western culture had changed and was continuing to change dramatically, church attendance was down, and the traditional use of scripture and ritual no longer held the same relevance that it had in the past. The profound influence of medicine, psychology, and technology compelled many to voice the need to uphold values of compassion, care, love, responsibility, and community, for example, as meaningful cultural, spiritual, and ethical guideposts. It was assumed that these values had been stripped from psychology, technology, and medicine. Further, it was assumed that the cultural shifts of the twentieth century, which also included great political and economic change, had produced a general spiritual distress manifested in expressions of meaninglessness, despair, and anxiety by those seeking psychological help and those who relied on the help of their church. What was advocated was the integration, not separation, in advances in psychological science with the spiritual realities of the population. This, it was assumed, would have a two-fold effect. First, psychology would acknowledge the need to expand its own interpretive tools from strictly scientific models of pathology and would come to address the human needs and aspirations of clients and patients. Second, religious leaders would acknowledge the great societal changes occurring in the twentieth century and adapt to meet the needs of their congregations and parishioners. Together, these interdisciplinary approaches to healthcare—psychological care, specifically—would not only benefit but force science to address the "whole" human being and not simply a biological or psychic entity interpreted and cured through a medical model of pathology.

In the West, we have come to assume that human existence should be fulfilling, that "normal" development exists, that it is attainable, and that psychotherapy in particular will facilitate this. These assumptions have been fueled by a variety of cultural factors. The prevalence of psychological theory and practice and medical advances and interventions have had an enormous impact on how we conceptualize our development. Our often unquestioning belief that psychology, for example, provides facts and givens about our existence has led us to believe that individually we have no personal responsibility in actively discovering and creating our fulfillment or, conversely, that societal and familial problems are the result of inner psychic processes and therefore not shared by all of us as a community. And yet what constitutes a fulfilling existence is both individually and culturally constructed, historically situated, politically motivated, and filled with ethical overlays and often religious subtext. The difficulties certain psychologists and theologians had with the scientism of psychology and its growing influence on Western society in the past remain with us today. Interdisciplinary dialogue during the mid-twentieth century seems equally pertinent today. Motivated to find what Erich Fromm described as a solidarity based on compassion and understanding, many within psychological, medical, and religious realms search for ways to unify the biological, psychological, and spiritual through compassion, responsibility, and care in the area of mental health, given our increasingly pluralistic, globalized, and often bewildering age.

Analyzing ideas, and interdisciplinary ones at that, is prone to theoretical complications. There is no one theory or systematic approach for convenient analysis. Exploring a vast subject such as health and well-being often produces more questions than answers and often muddies the waters with respect to which interpretive language we are using and whether we are favoring one interpretive lens over another. We do favor and interpret to make a point. My point is that in our present age, we are, once again, questioning the supremacy of psychology and medicine to interpret, diagnose, and guide human development. There is an increasing desire, especially by those who seek out therapy, to find a balance or unity between our biological, psychological, and spiritual selves. The importance currently given to the relationship between spirituality and mental health or spirituality and healing attests to this. Research, scholarship, and associations are increasingly emerging in order to expand our vision of what psychological health and development are. Integrative models of health care, which include addressing the spiritual resources of patients and the desire for more compassionate health care systems and medical models, further characterize this current trend. Once again, I would like to point out that this interest and these issues are not new. Further, such discussions tend to produce more questions than answers, but they do humble our work and remind us of Tillich's statement that "our very being is a continuous asking for the meaning of our being, a continuous attempt to decipher the enigma of our world and our heart."[9] I find such an attitude and approach meaningful, valuable, and highly creative. And despite the inherent theoretical complications, this kind of attitude has guided my own work and intellectual explorations for many years. The interdisciplinary emphasis on meaning, care, and responsibility has provided me with a positive and humane direction in which to approach teaching, therapy, and writing. I hope this book will generate further interest and deeper exploration by those scholars, and especially students, from a variety of disciplines who are motivated to question the fascinating ambiguities of the human condition.

[9] Tillich, "Knowledge Through Love," 111.

2

Paul Tillich and the New York Psychology Group, 1941 to 1945

Introduction

> We talk and talk and never listen to the voices speaking to our depth and from our depth. We accept ourselves as we appear to ourselves, and do not care what we really are. Like hit-and-run drivers, we injure our souls by the speed with which we move on the surface; and then we rush away, leaving our bleeding souls alone. We miss, therefore, our depth and our true life. And it is only when the picture that we have of ourselves breaks down completely, only when we find ourselves acting against all the expectations we had derived from that picture, and only when an earthquake shakes and disrupts the surface of our self-knowledge, that we are willing to look into a deeper level of our being.[1]

Paul Tillich made many astute and profound observations about human nature. The quotation that begins this chapter, taken from Tillich's famous collection of sermons *The Shaking of the Foundations*, was written during the years Tillich taught at New York's Union Theological Seminary (1933–1956). To what extent, Tillich asks, do we truly see ourselves, truly know ourselves? The assumptions we have about who we are and what we are capable of often mirror the certitude with which psychology and theology make claims about human nature. What happens, Tillich asks, when that certitude or seeming security is shaken or shattered? This quotation is fascinating in light of the discussions that took place between 1941 and 1945 in a casual monthly gathering known as the New York

---

[1] Paul Tillich, "The Depth of Existence" in *The Shaking of the Foundations* (New York: Charles Scribner's Sons: 1948) 56.

Psychology Group[2] (hereafter referred to as the NYPG). In the midst of the catastrophe of WWII, shaken and questioning the depth of change and uncertainty in the world, psychologists and theologians, many of whom were European émigrés, gathered together for interdisciplinary discussion. The intention of this chapter is to give an illustration of the questions and debates that both psychologists and theologians felt were necessary to discuss collaboratively given the context of global war, politics, and cultural change. These questions include a general assessment of the role of psychology itself and the limitations of both psychology and theology in analyzing human nature. Specifically, how does one analyze faith amidst chaos, how do we care for one another, and what are the differences between psychological and religious help? Much of the chapter focuses not so much on Tillich's direct contributions but rather on the intellectual perspectives and viewpoints that surrounded him for nearly five years. The legacy of these somewhat private discussions was, for Tillich, an enduring affiliation with interdisciplinary groups engaged in the dialogue between psychology and theology until his death in 1965.

---

[2] The New York Psychology Group of the National Council on Religion and Higher Education, 1941–1945. Very little is known about this group; even less is published. I wish to thank Prof. Allison Stokes of Ithaca College, New York, for providing Prof. Terry Cooper and me with the collective minutes and members' papers from this group, hereafter cited as NYPG. Prof. Stokes received these materials directly from Seward Hiltner, a prominent figure in pastoral counseling in the United States and founding member of the New York Psychology Group, who remained active in the group throughout its duration. Prof. Stokes published a chapter on the group entitled "Seward Hiltner, Paul Tillich and the New York Psychology Group" in her book *Ministry After Freud* (New York: Pilgrim Press, 1985). The chapter outlines the historical context for the group and provides biographical material on many of its prominent members. Brief mention that Tillich participated in the group also can be found in a footnote in Wilhelm and Marion Pauck's book *Paul Tillich: His Life and Thought* (New York: Harper & Row, 1976). Terry Cooper of the department of psychology at St. Louis Community College-Meremec presented a paper on the New York Psychology Group (based on the minutes and papers provided by Prof. Allison Stokes) to the North American Paul Tillich Society section of the American Academy of Religion's annual meeting in San Antonio, Texas, in November 2004. Cooper also devotes two excellent and extensive chapters to the entire minutes and papers of the New York Psychology Group in his book *Paul Tillich and Psychology: Historic and Contemporary Explorations in Theology, Psychotherapy, and Ethics* (Macon GA: Mercer University Press, 2006). I encourage those interested in this subject to read Dr. Cooper's book. I also would like to thank Dr. Cooper for our numerous conversations and collaborations regarding the NYPG.

Tillich's fascination with the discipline of psychology spanned decades. While he wrote frequently on the topic of psychology and the relation between psychology and theology, his interest in this interdisciplinary dialogue culminated in several fascinating intellectual associations. In addition to the New York Psychology Group, Tillich was involved with the Harvard Project on Religion and Mental Health from 1957 to 1961 and later the Academy of Religion and Mental Health, to name but two. Tillich also wrote extensively for the *Journal of Pastoral Psychology* and wrote several chapters in various publications on religion and mental health between 1957 and 1962. He served on the board of the Review of Existential Psychology and Psychiatry in the early 1960s and gave numerous lectures to psychological organizations. Tillich also had a long-standing association and friendship with American existential psychologist Rollo May.[3]

Although Tillich had been interested in psychology, particularly Freudian psychotherapy prior to WWII, Allison Stokes comments that "an intensified interest, knowledge, sensitivity and commitment to issues of religion and health, pastoral psychology, theology and counseling can be discerned in Tillich's post NYPG publications."[4] This intensified interest is further corroborated by Dr. Earl A. Loomis, Jr., a colleague of Tillich's at Union Theological Seminary, who made the following comment on Tillich's efforts to incorporate psychological theory into his own thinking:

> The effort to assimilate and accommodate himself to psychoanalysis was a difficult one for Tillich, as for many others of his time. Persisting, his

[3] Rollo May was a student of Tillich's at Union Seminary in New York. Tillich supervised May's doctoral dissertation, published in 1950 as *The Meaning of Anxiety* (New York: W. W. Norton & Company, 1977). May started attending sessions of the New York Psychology Group in the later years of its existence. There is much speculation as to whether Tillich's most psychologically oriented publication, *The Courage to Be* (New Haven CT: Yale University Press, 1980) was in fact written as an answer to Rollo May's book *The Meaning of Anxiety.* Although May claimed it was, many Tillich scholars disagree. There has been much speculation as to whether or not Tillich ever underwent any psychoanalytic treatment. During a lunch meeting with longtime Tillich friend Mrs. Jane Owen on 17 October 2003 in New Harmony, Indiana, (where Tillich is buried) I was informed that Tillich's wife, Hannah, had undergone a course of psychoanalysis with Rollo May, but Mrs. Owen was unsure whether Tillich himself had. Rollo May is said to have undergone a period of psychoanalysis with fellow NYPG member Erich Fromm.

[4] Stokes, *Ministry After Freud*, 118.

> curiosity eventually was rewarded and the interchange that grew out of his close alliance with analysis and analytic thought was enduring. In time he came to speak and write as one who had seen the problems and the conflicts, one who had experienced the drives and defenses, one who had struggled with the resistances and the transference. Eventually the familiarity became deep and lasting.[5]

In addition to the numerous articles, book chapters, and active working associations Tillich had with psychology following WWII, his continued influence on contemporary psychological theory attests to the wide interest and relevance of his thought.[6] Chapters 5 and 6 provide further illustrations of Tillich's relevance to contemporary theory. In these two chapters I superimpose Tillich's thought on critical psychology and existential analysis.

Between 1941 and 1945, however, the NYPG was a forum in which Tillich listened to, absorbed, debated, and analyzed questions and issues that arose amidst dialogue between psychology and theology. While the NYPG met for nearly five years and included an illustrious membership, very little is known about the group, the discussions that took place, or the significance of such a gathering. Tillich was on faculty at Union Theological Seminary during the years the group met, and his participation in the group represented his first serious engagement in this kind of interdisciplinary dialogue after arriving in the United States. So much of Tillich's later writings and sermons, for both psychological and theological audiences, would reflect deep and profoundly astute observations about human existence. Although much of that astuteness came from Tillich's own personal struggles,[7] in addition to his always considering himself on

---

[5] Ibid.

[6] Perry Lefevre's book *The Meaning of Health: Essays in Existentialism, Psychoanalysis, and Religion* (Chicago: Exploration Press, 1984) is an edited selection from Tillich's vast number of published articles on the topic of psychology and theology. In addition to the many references existential psychologist Rollo May makes in his books to Tillich's thought, Kirk J. Schneider's *Rediscovery of Awe* (St. Paul MN: Paragon House, 2004) and Robert A. Emmons's *The Psychology of Ultimate Concerns* (New York: Guilford Press, 1999) are just a few examples of Tillich's continued relevance and influence on contemporary psychological writers and theorists.

[7] I thank Matthew Lon Weaver, member of the North American Paul Tillich Society and editor along with Ron Stone of *Against the Third Reich: Paul Tillich's Wartime Radio Broadcasts into Nazi Germany* (Louisville KY: Westminster John Knox Press, 1998), for our many conversations over the years about Tillich's role as military

the boundary intellectually with several disciplines, one can trace strong influences from the NYPG in many later writings and associations with psychologists. Reading through the minutes and papers of this group, one is struck by how little Tillich actually spoke. His regular attendance, though, and the comments he did contribute during meetings leave one with the very strong sense that Tillich was keenly present and soaking in everything that was being said.

The depth of the questions raised and the answers debated among the psychologists and theologians of the NYPG represent a remarkable illustration of interdisciplinary discussion. Not only do these materials provide a valuable contribution to the history of religion and mental health in the United States, the conversations that took place during the NYPG meetings also explore some profoundly important issues that continue to resonate today about the role of psychology and what, in fact, constitutes psychological health and development. Further, members of this informal

---

chaplain in Germany during WWI and his subsequent emotional breakdowns during that time. Further, Tillich's daughter, Dr. Mutie Tillich Farris, has claimed that her father suffered post-traumatic stress disorder following WWI, a state, she feels, he never fully recovered from. Tillich often spoke of his experience witnessing the deaths of friends during WWI. In later years, he would suggest that these experiences opened his eyes forever and made him even more acutely aware of our capacity for destruction. Yet Tillich always believed in our creative potential and came to see these two very human tendencies (realities) residing side by side in each of us. Tillich's positioning of human development, potential, and psychological health in the middle of these polarities brought his "psychological" thinking into close alignment with the existential psychotherapies. Although highly controversial amongst Tillich scholars, Hannah Tillich's publication of *From Time to Time* (New York: Stein & Day, 1973) also makes reference to Tillich's psychological distress after WWI. In that book, she discusses Tillich's keen interest in psychology, his friendships over the years with psychologists, and his increased participation in psychological organizations during the years he lived in the United States. Dr. Mutie Tillich Farris shared with me her mother's great interest in psychology, an interest Dr. Farris believes preceded her father's. Her mother's interest, like that of many Europeans at the time, mirrored the burgeoning field of psychoanalysis, and Dr. Farris said her mother adopted the psychological parlance of the day. Further, Hannah Tillich would often engage her husband in discussions on psychology and psychological theory. Paul Tillich's interest in psychology grew substantially following the family's emigration to the United States in the early 1930s. Dr. Farris recalls the extent to which her parents socialized and entertained psychologists at their home, including her own memories of her father in animated conversation with psychoanalyst Karen Horney at the family dinner table. I would like to thank Dr. Farris for sharing this information with me during two telephone conversations I had with her in September and December 2006.

yet illustrious monthly gathering were acutely aware of world events and the impact these events had on discussions about human nature and development. Many of the discussions centered on the necessity and value, if not urgency, of this particular interdisciplinary dialogue in light of these events. Members also debated which side—psychology or theology—was better equipped to deal with the effects global changes were having on individuals. In the final year of the group's meetings, Dr. Grace Elliott described the necessity of theologians and psychologists coming together not only to learn from each other, but also, perhaps, to place what she called "the real perplexities in our own fields"[8] into greater context.

Bringing psychologists and theologians together amidst the backdrop of WWII fostered further discussions about ethics, social responsibility, human nature, love, and the care for others. Members of the NYPG often described the period in which they were living as desperate. Whether they were theologians or psychologists, there was a unanimous belief that the world was undergoing rapid and profound change. The results, they felt, were visible and increased signs of anxiousness, apathy, and a sense of meaninglessness among the population. These psychological and spiritual signs of change were witnessed in therapy sessions and amongst congregations. A growing sub-text running through the group's discussions was that institutions and ideologies that had seemingly provided social, and by extension, personal stability, in the past were now crumbling. As Tillich suggests in the opening quotation to this chapter, It is "only when an earthquake shakes and disrupts the surface of our self-knowledge that we are willing to look into a deeper level of our being." Members of the NYPG were not engaging in passive intellectualizing; the discussions reveal shifts and struggles with personal ideology and a desire for action.

Members often conveyed, as mentioned, a sense of urgency about the time in which they were living, and that meant realistically assessing what psychologists and ministers could provide in these "desperate" times. Dr. Grace Elliott stated,

[8] Minutes of the New York Psychology Group, 9 February 1945. I am relying on the date of discussion to document quotes from members because the full minutes and papers of the NYPG are organized by year and not numbered by page.

> In these desperate days [he] has a new urgency to [his] ever present question, Why was I born? What is the meaning of life? How can I discover it? But [he] cannot be given that answer as a legacy, a gift, a favor—even from God. [He] has to find it, achieve it, work it out for himself. [He] cannot escape that responsibility.... My quarrel with the theologians is that too often they have paid little attention to the process, that they have thought they could preach or exhort or argue or persuade men and women into the Kingdom of Heaven. On the other hand my quarrel with the psychiatrists is that too often they won't admit that [man] cannot be whole without finding for [himself] those values, those goals, and that sense of direction which give meaning to life and security for its risks. Those helped by them may be all dressed up with no place to go, while the minister's clients know where to go but haven't any idea how to get there. We must work together both on goals and on understanding the conditions for their achievement.[9]

As we will see in later chapters, comments such as these are fascinating in light of the philosophic and therapeutic approach Viktor Frankl presented to the United States a decade or so later, and they resonate profoundly with Alfried Längle's contemporary theory of Existential Analysis. Members of the New York Psychology Group assumed that fostering dialogue between psychology and theology was not only necessary to better grasp human development and potential, but that it was also necessary for responsible action in the world. Assuming the inextricable link between individual and social or cultural development, the group's members, particularly the most vocal—Erich Fromm and Seward Hiltner—reflected their own intellectual backgrounds and influence from groups such as the Frankfurt School of critical theory in the 1920s and the pastoral counseling movement in the United States. This sense of social urgency assumed that both psychologists and theologians had active, integrative roles to play.

Throughout this book, the problem with psychology, and its perceived limited scope, is illustrated in the various dialogues between those involved in the fields of psychology and theology that took place mid-twentieth century in the United States. Underlying so many of these dialogues was a view of human nature as complex, ambiguous, and requiring an interdisciplinary lens for appropriate study. Further,

---

[9] Ibid.

underneath these larger questions about human existence, we see illustrations of the impact the integration of psychological theory and education had on theologians and seminaries. While many theologians, like Tillich, made genuine efforts to integrate psychological perspectives into their theological language, many also began a critical examination of the degree to which psychology could effectively analyze and answer questions about human nature. The critical examination of psychology would be taken up again, albeit from different perspectives, by humanistic and existentially oriented psychologists during the late 1950s and 1960s, and would reemerge in the last two decades in postmodern approaches, such as critical psychology and contemporary existential psychotherapy. In the 1940s, theologians who engaged in this kind of interdisciplinary dialogue were well aware of psychology's growing influence and on one level were keen to integrate psychological and social scientific advances into their own perspectives on human nature. On a very practical level, many involved in pastoral counseling and training in seminaries were eager to upgrade or modernize approaches to counseling in order to provide prospective ministers with more relevant therapeutic tools when dealing with parishioners.[10] On the other hand, many were assessing the impact psychological theory had on society in general and questioned whether a scientific and methodological approach (often referred to in the NYPG group as a "deterministic approach") to human nature could effectively analyze issues of faith, meaning, values, and ethics. Indeed, many questioned whether psychology could effectively analyze existential questions at all. Which side was better equipped to deal with these, or was there some common ground between the two? When the NYPG began meeting in 1941, the psychologists and theologians within this unique group were in agreement that an interdisciplinary dialogue was the most

[10] This was a very interesting development. As we will see in chapter 4, the influence of psychology and therapeutic models on seminary school curriculum and church leaders blurred the distinctions between religious and psychological problems. Further, the adaptation of therapeutic "tools" assumed an interpretive, almost diagnostic approach to individuals and the "problems" they presented. This muddied the waters even further as to whether theologians were adopting psychology as science or whether they were integrating and therefore framing psychological perspectives and therapeutic approaches in what NYPG member and theologian David E. Roberts would later call another form of human fellowship that dealt with moral problems.

fruitful approach. The desire was to restructure theoretical passivity into possible concrete action at the therapeutic and ministerial levels.

The New York Psychology Group: 1941 to 1945

Because very little is known about the New York Psychology Group, it is difficult to fully reflect on its importance based on the materials available. The minutes and paper presentations from the group's meetings do, however, warrant serious attention, and much more scholarly work needs to be done to analyze the various contexts that influenced the group's creation and the substance of their debates.[11] It is somewhat surprising, given the illustrious membership and the dedicated interest members had in the intersection between psychology and theology, that so little is known about the NYPG. Founding member Seward Hiltner recalls an informal agreement among members not to discuss the meetings, although this did not imply that the meetings were considered private. Further, existential psychologist Rollo May, who was a graduate student at Union Theological Seminary when he joined the group, would later comment during interviews with Allison Stokes that it was only in hindsight that the importance and significance of the group's meetings and discussions became apparent.[12] The following six general comments about the group provide insights.

First, the NYPG was founded by Seward Hiltner, who was widely known in pastoral counseling circles, and social psychologist Erich Fromm. The NYPG's membership, by invitation only, was comprised of psychologists, psychoanalysts, medical doctors, theologians, and graduate students. Many members were on faculty at Union Theological Seminary or Columbia University, and many others were Freudian or Jungian

[11] As stated, Terry Cooper and I hope our interest and attention to the NYPG will generate a desire by other scholars to explore this group and the materials even further. Cooper gives an excellent and full account of NYPG discussions in his book. I have drawn out several key themes related to the meaning of health and well-being.

[12] Stokes, *Ministry After Freud*, 113. Stokes interviewed both Seward Hiltner and Rollo May when she was conducting research for her book. Stokes points out that Rollo May never mentions Tillich's participation in the group (I assume she is referring to May's book *Paulus* [Dallas TX: Saybrook, 1988]). Hannah Tillich, who was present with her husband at every one of the NYPG meetings, is also silent about Tillich's participation in the group in her book *From Time to Time* (New York: Stein & Day, 1973).

analysts in private practice in New York. Prominent members included theologian and hospital chaplain Otis Rice; theologian and pastoral counselor Seward Hiltner; Paul Tillich, of course; and fellow Union Seminary professors David E. Roberts and Thomas Bigham. The psychiatrist Gotthard Booth and social psychologist Erich Fromm were joined by the humanistic psychologists Carl Rogers and Rollo May, Freudian analysts Ernest Schachtel and Greta Frankley, and Jungian analysts Frances Wickes and Martha Glickman. Membership in the group changed somewhat from year to year, but the members mentioned here represent a portion of the core group that remained intact throughout the period 1941 to 1945.

Many members of the NYPG were European émigrés who brought an array of familial, cultural, political, religious, and educational backgrounds to bear on the monthly discussions, especially in light of the war raging in Europe. Stokes identifies the NYPG among the "liberal intelligensia [*sic*]"[13] rising in the United States at the time. "Liberal intellectuals maintained that sharing human diversity offered a more authentic, reliable, and satisfying perspective than did narrow parochialism."[14] Stokes adds, "The one thing group members held surely in common was their liberal, intellectual style of thought. Indeed, if the secular liberal intelligensia [*sic*] can be said to have had a *religious* counterpart in these years, most members of the NYPG belonged to it, and Tillich, Hiltner, Roberts, and May were among its nationally prominent leaders."[15] Within this liberal group, members of the NYPG represented secular and religious (both Christian and Jewish) perspectives, in addition to a variety of professions and theoretical positions. Women comprised a large number of the prominent members. Not only was the group distinctive in bringing psychology and theology together in discussion, the strong membership of professional female analysts further attests to this striking group.

Second, Allison Stokes has suggested that the group should be seen as an important historical contribution to what is very loosely referred to as the religion and mental health movement that took place mid-twentieth century in the United States. Indeed, many members would continue to be

---

[13] Ibid., 136.

[14] Ibid., 137.

[15] Ibid., 138.

affiliated with similar interdisciplinary groups for several decades to follow. Founding NYPG members Seward Hiltner and theologian Paul Tillich, for example, would later be involved in the Harvard Project on Religion and Mental Health beginning in 1957 and then as members of the Academy of Religion and Mental Health in the early 1960s. Reverends Otis Rice and Thomas Bingham would also become involved in the Academy of Religion and Mental Health. Gotthard Booth, M.D., became involved in the Harvard Project on Religion and Mental Health and contributed chapters in several books published in the late 1950s on the subject of religion and health.[16] As Stokes reflected, "That these particular individuals met at this particular historical moment is a fact of incalculable importance for the growth of religion and health. What had been a small movement before the war blossomed beyond expectation in the postwar era, partly as a result of their intellectual effort and influence."[17] Further, "The New York Psychology Group essentially functioned not to break new conceptual ground, but to explore the interrelation of religion and health by providing a forum for intellectual exchange and fellowship."[18]

Third, the group's discussions are not only an important illustration of interdisciplinary dialogue between psychology and theology, they illustrate how such dialogues are grounded in and influenced by historical and cultural context. Blending two perspectives to discuss human nature and human development was influenced both by world events and a sense of global urgency. Stokes writes, "The world war was ever a part of the group's consciousness...their experience of disruption [many being European émigrés] and displacement intensified the group's awareness of global warfare and strengthened the predominant sense that intelligent and informed discussion of the relationship between depth psychology and theology was urgent."[19]

---

[16] Booth contributed chapters, for example, in two works edited by Simon Doniger, *Religion and Health* (New York: Association Press, 1958) and *Healing: Human and Divine* (New York: Association Press, 1957). These publications also include contributions from original NYPG members Paul Tillich, Seward Hiltner, and Carl Rogers.

[17] Stokes, *Ministry After Freud*, 115.

[18] Ibid., 113.

[19] Ibid., 117.

Fourth, from a theological and pastoral counseling perspective, Seward Hiltner would later comment to Allison Stokes that the rapid rise of psychology and secular counseling had an impact not only on the role and nature of pastoral counseling but that psychology's rise in importance would increasingly impact the "therapeutic" obligation ministers and pastors were increasingly requested to dispense. Interestingly, the rise and integration of psychological theory, language, and terminology meant that the therapeutic intervention undertaken by a minister or pastor would be scrutinized more carefully under this new psychological perspective;[20] scrutinized more carefully by those in charge of seminary schools as well as parishioners, who themselves were increasingly influenced by, and internalizing, this new language and its perspectives on human nature, behavior, and emotion. A prevailing perception of secular psychology's growing influence on culture was absorbed within theological and pastoral counseling circles. The psychological lens of "scrutiny," as Seward describes, would continue well into the 1950s, when Hans Hofmann of the Harvard Divinity School became head of the Harvard Project on Religion and Mental Health and placed a priority on addressing not only the kind of psychological training ministers and pastors received in seminary schools but also the kind of personal psychological analysis ministerial students were expected to undergo and complete in order to better serve (therapeutically) their parishioners, and by extension, the community.

Fifth, the NYPG did not have a set mandate nor was it affiliated to a specific university, religious, or government institution. Although many of the theologians in the group, for example, were on faculty at Union Seminary and reflected a strong politically liberal and Protestant stance, the group discussions were not guided by any specific external body. The informality of the group's discussions is apparent when one reads through the minutes. The material is profoundly rich and yet sometimes confusing, the debates both riveting and disorganized. Amidst the contradictions in arguments made by members throughout the years, one detects a strong and natural progression of shifting positions, a real working through, both intellectually and personally, some fairly profound questions about human nature, capability, and potential. It is precisely this character—the

[20] Ibid., 109.

combination of theoretical debate and personal sentiment—that makes the minutes of the NYPG so compelling.

Sixth, given the rather illustrious cast of characters and their respective contributions to psychology and theology, there are numerous ways and approaches with which one could analyze the material. What is most striking is the constant, often overwhelming, number of questions raised by its participants. It would seem that the group provided a nonjudgmental arena to ask profound questions about existence and about the strengths and weaknesses of both psychology and theology without the feeling that answers necessarily needed to be provided. One gets a sense, in fact, of the enthusiasm participants had for the process itself, a profound sentiment that an open questioning without too many theoretical boundaries could provide much creative food for thought. And the material does just that.

Introducing the Discussions

Members of the NYPG took turns hosting the monthly meetings. During the years 1941 to 1945, the group's meetings and subsequent discussions were organized around four themes: the psychology of faith, the psychology of love, the psychology of conscience, and the psychology of help, also known as the function of psychological help. Each meeting began with a preselected paper given by a member. These presentations were then followed by an open discussion among all members present. Tillich attended nearly all the meetings during these years and gave three papers: "The Concept of Faith in the Jewish-Christian Tradition" (1942), "Fragments of an Ontology of Love" (1943), and "Conscience—Historical and Typological Remarks" (1943).

The four main themes provided overall structure, but discussions frequently centered on the relationship between ethics and psychotherapy. Was psychoanalysis in the "business of ethics"? In other words, were psychological categories of health and healthy development also ethical statements on human behavior and conduct? This question was hotly debated, with Tillich emphatically claiming that it certainly was, while other members, specifically psychologists, claiming that psychology had no business being engaged in ethics. Other debated issues centered on the difference between the ethics an individual adopted versus the ethics an individual lived by in conjunction with the wider society he or she inhabited. The following statement, given by a member during a meeting in 1944, conveys the idea that our individual experiences and notions of mental health and inner fulfillment are inextricably linked to social frameworks and collectively shared notions of human conduct and behavior: "A person's ethical achievements and judgments are set within a framework which is not completely at [his] own disposal, so that wisdom, mental health, inner peace for every individual are partly dependent upon [his] own initiative and partly upon [his] coming to terms cooperatively with structures and truths that [he] did not create and does not sustain by any effort of [his] will..."[21]

Further, many questions that the group raised sound surprisingly familiar in today's therapeutic settings: Were there differences, for example, in the therapeutic approach based on the religious, social, or cultural context of the client? What was the aim of psychotherapy, and what were the implications of theory and therapy beyond the individual? What were the expectations of the client? What kind of "help" did they want and feel they needed? What, by extension, was the client internalizing about the process and the nature of therapy itself?

Underneath the discussions, and despite the commentary by one member that "values" were not at play in the mandate of the group, the NYPG was, in fact, advocating an "ultimate concern," to borrow a Tillichian phrase, for the welfare of all. Within the interdisciplinary and intellectual nature of the discussions, a 1943 meeting debated whether an ideological concept advocating the unity of humankind could develop into a reality.[22] One can easily argue, as we shall see in chapter 5, that these same questions of ultimate concern dominate many contemporary discussions in psychology, albeit without reference to or dialogue with history or religion.

During the years the NYPG met, natural shifts occurred in the emphasis members placed on either psychological or theological perspectives. The meetings during the first year focused on discussions about the psychology of faith and heavily favored, not surprisingly, a psychological and social scientific approach, if not bias, toward the issue of faith. During the group's final year in 1945, however, discussions about

---

[21] Dr. David E. Roberts, NYPG, 14 January 1944.

[22] General discussion, NYPG, 4 June 1943.

the psychology of help were far more philosophical. They addressed psychology's perceived limitations to deal with issues concerning the meaning and value of human existence in addition to the recognition that those seeking therapeutic intervention often were seeking direction, counsel, wisdom, and guidance on issues that were not necessarily categories of psychic illness but, instead, profound questions of existence.

Also of interest, given the historical context and world events of the time, is the general tone of the group's discussions. Discussions often were dominated by contrasts of positive and negative behavior, and an underlying subtext advocating universal values—positive ones at that—is quite apparent. Whether members spoke from a psychological or theological perspective, the group frequently formulated discussions around such issues as love, responsibility, freedom, relation, community, solidarity, the differences between individual and cultural development, and ethics. Always questioning whether such topics could be presented as universal human capacities, if not essential, the group discussed what could be seen as ideals of human progress. Therefore, normal or rational faith was contrasted with "pseudo-rational" faith and emphasis was placed on being able to clearly identify what was rational faith and what was irrational. Positive and creative behavior went up against possessive and destructive behavior. Healthy expressions of solidarity and community were contrasted with irrational authority or possessive, destructive, and dominating power.

While members within the psychology camp often emphatically distinguished their own discipline as a relatively value-free enterprise from theology, which was labeled value-laden, the group as a whole was generally in agreement about ideal directions for human progress and psychological and spiritual health. These themes, once again, were predominantly love, solidarity, community, freedom, and responsibility. The question was how could these "positives," these valued ideals, be reinforced in psychology at the individual level and theology at a more societal level, and, further, how could they be internalized by the general population. The assumption was that if these valued ideals could be clearly identified, upheld, and expressed both individually and culturally, the world would be a better place. Could psychology and theology together bring this about?

What follows is a summary of the open-ended questions that marked the debates amongst members, particularly during the "psychology of faith" meetings that took place between December 1941 and May 1942 and the "psychology of help" meetings held between October 1944 and March 1945. Of importance to this thesis is the fact that many of these questions continued in discussions between psychologists and theologians through the 1950s and early 1960s and have reemerged in postmodern theories as critical psychology and contemporary therapeutic approaches, such as Alfried Längle's Existential Analysis. Equally important to this book is that theologian Paul Tillich was deeply influenced by these discussions. They serve to place in context Tillich's continued interest in psychology, the impact this had on his subsequent writings about human nature, and why contemporary scholars in psychology continue to call upon his thought.

The Psychology of Faith

The opening session of the New York Psychology Group took place on 5 December 1941. Having established that the first series of meetings from December 1941 to May 1942 would discuss the psychology of faith, the group introduced its first open questions for debate: Could faith be considered an attitude of the whole personality? Was our subjective experience of faith different from faith in God? Could faith be validly explored from biological, sociological, and psychological perspectives? Was the content of one's faith linked to the culture of which one is a part? More specifically, was faith an inherent part of human life? "If there is life," Seward Hiltner asked, "is there faith"[23]? Did faith presume action? In other words, if one had faith, would one act, and, perhaps more importantly, would that act be positive and creative? Did faith, in other words, presume human potentialities for virtuous behavior and action? Was faith best studied from the standpoint of emotion? Was faith the deepest level of emotion? How much consideration needed to be given to the "object" of one's faith? Could variations in faith be distinguished? Could one clearly distinguish between rational or genuine faith and what Erich Fromm called "pseudo"[24] or irrational faith?

In the meetings that followed, these ideas and questions were explored further. The questions that framed the first sessions were, as mentioned, predominantly psychological. Many of the questions were placed in the

---

[23] NYPG, 5 December 1941.

[24] NYPG, 5 December 1941.

context of personality structure, emotions, and the ability to observe and categorize not so much the object of one's faith but faith as object. The following is worth highlighting from the first year the NYPG met: the idea of faith as an attitude; that faith is related to social structures versus divine realms; and that faith implies interdependence, an I/thou relation.

Faith was discussed as a specific attitude of the whole personality. At the subjective level, faith, and rational faith at that, was described from the standpoint of personality structure. Mirroring in many ways characteristics of psychological health, psychologists in the group discussed faith in terms of the specific characteristics an individual would possess. These included firmness in one's state of mind, certainty, balance, dignity, integrity, courage, the ability to love, steadfastness, and freedom. Psychologists in the group contended that an individual who possessed these internal characteristics was likely to experience the world as positive. Further, these positive and "healthy" personality traits, they believed, predisposed an individual to adopting an attitude of faith and hope about human beings and the world itself. The psychologists within the group redirected theological discussions about the object of one's faith or receiving the ability for faith through a divine source to an emphasis on human capability and experience based on internal characteristics, personality structure, and attitude. Erich Fromm reiterated his secular psychological position stating that rational faith "is one where the weight is upon the active experience of the individual and not on his receiving the gift of grace from God or any authority."[25]

While Fromm, like many other psychologists within the group, placed rational faith within the confines of individual personality structure, there was an underlying assumption that an individual who possessed these psychologically healthy characteristics was essentially free and responsible and would carry the right attitude out into the world. Faith derived from a healthy personality structure engendered the right attitude that assumed, in turn, right action. This position is interesting in light of the dialogues between psychology and theology to come in the decades that followed. On the heels of the Harvard Project on Religion and Mental Health (1957 to 1961), the Rev. Harry C. Meserve of the Academy of Religion and Mental Health outlined the characteristics of a healthy

---

[25] NYPG, 20 May 1942.

"religious" person. These included "a realistic attitude towards the tribulations of the world" and an approach toward people and the world generally that was "expectant and hopeful, rather than critical and negative."[26]

In summary, given the heavy emphasis on psychological interpretation in the first year the NYPG met, faith did not lead to psychological health; rather, psychological health and wholeness predisposed an individual attitudinally to the right kind of faith and rational faith specifically. This healthy individual, embodying an attitude of faith, would, it was assumed, act justly and ethically in the world.

In the final meeting of the first year in May 1942, several comments were made about faith in external social structures and ideologies. With the events in Europe clearly on the minds of members present, Erich Fromm stated that he believed rational faith could not be faith in evil.[27] In his opinion, stating that one had faith in the ideologies of a political dictatorship, for example, was not rational faith. Ruth Benedict took Fromm's comment one step further at this same meeting and asked the provocative question of whether faith was even possible "when the social order is chaotic."[28] In other words, was an individual even capable of an attitude of faith if the external world in which the individual participated and was influenced by was not itself stable? How stable were these internal personality traits? Weighing the influence of and link between the social world and the individual, Benedict answered her own question by suggesting that there were, in fact, distinctions between personal and social experiences of faith and that examples could always be drawn in which individuals exhibited faith despite difficult circumstances or occasions of social chaos and upheaval. This commentary is interesting given Viktor Frankl's position after the war about an individual's capacity to adopt a unique and profoundly personal attitude based on individual freedom and decision in moments of great tragedy, turmoil, and despair. The NYPG materials provide fascinating glimpses into an ongoing debate about whether or not there are essential human characteristics, the degree to which

---

[26] Richard V. McCann, *The Churches and Mental Health* (New York: Basic Books, 1962) 6.

[27] NYPG, 20 May 1942.

[28] NYPG, 20 May 1942.

we are self-made, socially constructed, or a complex combination of all three.

Rational faith also assumed relation. Faith involved both the internal and highly subjective attitudes and emotions of the individual but simultaneously was directed toward an object, and that, in turn, implied the relational quality of faith, although the psychologists continued to deny any theological similarity with a human/divine relation. Harry Bone made the following comments during the February 1942 meeting:

[Faith] is experiencing life with one's whole self, as worth living. It is the normal and inevitable outlook of a healthy personality; that is, one who is realizing in significant degree [his] whole self, sensuous, emotional, intellectual. This faith in the structure of life, faith in the possibilities of human nature, faith in one's fellows, faith in oneself, faith in life, faith in the world—are all aspects of one indivisible life attitude.[29]

The attitude Bone spoke of—an open attitude of faith in the possibilities of human capability, the possibilities of human relation, and community—was taken up by Erich Fromm when he stated that "the essential problem of [man] is not that of frustration and satisfaction of needs but of [his] relatedness to others in the world and the necessity thereof. Otherwise, [he] dies spiritually, i.e. becomes insane."[30] Rational faith was not only an internal subjective experience, rational faith prompted positive, relational experiences in the world. Further, an attitude of faith in our human potential made a positive statement about community and fellowship, and this was linked once again to psychological health and development. Individuals needed relation to be healthy. Unconsciously, many psychologists in the group were, in fact, advocating a philosophical stance about faith in community, in each other, in life itself, and attempting to link positive community and relational action as a criterion for psychological health.

For Harry Bone, having faith that life itself was worthwhile and meaningful meant that the world was experienced and perceived subjectively as supportive, stable, and reliable. Once again, this concept sparked numerous debates as to whether we inherently have faith and belief in a structure of reality prior to our immediate subjective experience and

---

[29] NYPG, 6 February 1942.

[30] NYPG, 6 February 1942.

experiences of the social structures that surround us, especially when those structures are chaotic and destructive. Members debated "where the future trend of faith [would] go."[31] Reflecting the global instability of the time, Elizabeth Rohrbach suggested, "Where faith has torn loose from old symbols, something else has risen up to take their place, i.e. the state, the supernatural."[32] Members discussed the shifts occurring to the cultural and personal symbols of relatedness. Did human beings deliberately orient themselves toward these symbols or, once again, were our experiences of relatedness the foundation upon which faith and trust were born? Seeing faith as possibly unstable, of being "torn loose," implied that there was no stable source of relatedness, and one can sense within these discussions personal struggles of faith taking place within members who were simultaneously attempting to analyze the world situation.

According to theologian David E. Roberts, though, faith would necessarily fix on something that symbolized relatedness,[33] and this relatedness would be perceived and experienced as supportive and trustworthy. As Rollo May commented during the May 1942 meeting,

> To understand who this individual is who is free and spontaneous, we must consider this individual's relatedness to something other than [himself]. Certainly [he] must be related to [his] fellow man. Beyond that [he] must be related to some structure of meaning. [He] is spontaneous as [he] is able to express in [himself] the reality of human experience more than the immediate situation. We reach the religious when we move beyond the culturally conditioned individual to the structure of reality, the universe in which he lives.[34]

May presumed that human beings have the capacity to express, and indeed are always expressing, a reality that transcends the immediate, the tangible, and the explainable. Raising once again the possibility of a structure of meaning symbolizing relatedness that was prior to our immediate senses, May's opinion, like that of many NYPG members, reflects very personal and professional alliances. May's combined existential

[31] David E. Roberts, 6 February 1942.
[32] NYPG, 6 March 1942.
[33] NYPG, 6 February 1942.
[34] NYPG, 20 May 1942.

psychotherapeutic and theological position is clear in his statements about what lies beyond our immediate senses and knowledge.

Although members often agreed in general discussions, differences between theologians and psychologists appeared rapidly when they came close to conclusions. Fromm suggested that "the church had essentially failed in providing a symbolic expression of the solidarity of [men]."[35] Different symbolic forms would emerge, Fromm contended, and what might very well emerge was "a society of [mankind] in which the solidarity of [men] would find expression in the social organization."[36] In a later meeting, however, Harry Bone would counter Fromm's own "faith" in social organizations by suggesting that our limitations as human beings "are often rooted in the social structure and become part of our own mental equipment. Rather than think in terms of society or culture as some entity, the point is that if one takes social solidarity seriously, [his] faith has to be limited, or the problem of achieving it has to be limited, by the situation of all [his] fellows."[37] This point raised the familiar issue about whether faith developed from an experience of trust in a structure of reality that was prior to social organizations we actively create.

What is interesting is that in either case, taking theological or secular psychological positions, members of the NYPG collectively conveyed the idea that faith was a belief in certain ethical principles and fundamental human ideals. When discussions turned to the question of whether or not there was a difference between "faith as a human attitude" and "faith in God," Paul Tillich stated that he did not believe "that the alternative was between God and self-discovery."[38] Tillich continued,

> If one describes the existential situation of [man], one cannot do it all in inner psychological terms, because the very character of the existential self is standing face to face with our ultimate meaning under the threat and fear of losing one's existence. Even if we go as far as possible with those who say that faith is the discovery of self, the element of discovering something beyond one's self is involved.[39]

---

[35] NYPG, 6 March 1942.
[36] Ibid.
[37] NYPG, 20 March 1942.
[38] NYPG, 9 January 1942.
[39] Ibid.

Tillich suggested that what we must do is symbolize our inner experiences, but then what would the right symbols be? The symbols, Tillich believed, had to express something ultimate and unconditioned as opposed to ordinary and conditioned, and the criteria would be universality.

These discussions extended to lengthy debates over concepts of self, spontaneity, attitude, and freedom. Members discussed the inherent difficulty in defining any of these terms and how they could be applied. Harry Bone aptly suggested that these discussions "remind us that the real issues of life are not verbal and intellectual—they are problems of action involving the whole personality."[40] Rollo May continued to argue his position in later meetings that defining faith from a centered self was difficult because "faith in one's self and in others involves faith in a structure of reality."[41] The idea that faith and trust is contingent upon our experience of a structure of reality that holds or binds us was furthered by Grace Elliott, who suggested that we also depend on such a structure. The experiences of both dependence and trust lead to our ability to be spontaneous, to let ourselves go and respond freely with an attitude that corresponds to a centered and authentic self.[42] In other words, a positive attitude of faith toward self and world that engenders ethical and relational behavior naturally flows from experiences of dependence and trust.

Whether this "structure of reality" was identified as God or left ambiguous, Tillich saw the reality of human existence as ambiguous and paradoxical because of the circular character of faith itself. Faith for human beings, according to Tillich, was, in part, an acceptance of this ambiguous reality. Faith was an experience of union in spite of the ambiguity (the ambiguity of dependence and trust, of individual and social experience) and not an overcoming of this reality of human existence. "Faith," Tillich stated, "implies the experience of a paradoxical, transcendent, unconditioned order, which to accept is the fulfillment of our being."[43] Faith as union, despite the paradoxical nature of human existence, had a transforming quality to it. Much like the psychologists in the group,

[40] NYPG, 20 March 1942.

[41] NYPG, 20 March 1942.

[42] Grace Elliott, NYPG, 20 March 1942.

[43] Paul Tillich, "The Concept of Faith in the Jewish Christian Tradition" (paper presented at the meeting of the NYPG in New York on 10 April 1942).

Tillich equated faith with an act of acceptance and attitude inextricably related to health and healing. Healing, for Tillich, was living in the paradoxical order. To say that one's life was fulfilling was to accept the unity of finiteness and infinity, the paradoxical unity of reality and possibility.

For Tillich, psychology was the "context of the conditioned relation, the earthly, immanent experiences of our soul."[44] He believed this context limited psychology because healing and the positive development of humankind resided in the midst of our human capacity for faith and symbolism, or the capacity to experience moments of psychological unity within experiences of faith and acceptance. "Being," Tillich commented, "has always some mystery in it which cannot be expressed in scientific terms or anthropological terms or ethical terms and appears in manifestations of symbolic character—love, justice, truth, etc."[45] Where would love and freedom, in their unconditioned character, as Tillich referred to it, be rooted if not in immediate and conditioned social structures?

As the first year of meetings came to a close, it was obvious that discussions of faith, whether related to individual experience, conditioned by social structures, or alluding to a transcendent or religious realm, all took place in the context of catastrophic world events. Is it any wonder, then, that much discussion was spent on distinguishing authentic from irrational faith? This context informed the groups' definition of rational faith, with its ideals of healthy personality, ideals of relation, community, fellowship, and love. Faith, regardless of the disciplinary bias, meant positive action and ethical behavior. Amidst the divisions between psychologists and theologians over social versus divine realms, all the members advocated a strong universal faith that is clearly evident and succinctly summarized by Martha Glickman in spring 1942:

> If each were to examine the reasons why [he] came into the group and spent so much time and effort, it would not be a question of faith in certain values nor of whether [he] believed in God or not. It would rather be to gather insights from all of these divergent points of view to implement [his] faith in this critical hour in which we are living. But we

---

[44] Ibid.

[45] NYPG, 20 May 1942.

must not rest content with discussion; the possibilities of activation are many and varied.[46]

Glickman assumed that faith was an essential human characteristic and expression that both psychologists and theologians took for granted. The members of the New York Psychology Group, each shaken by world events yet sustained through dialogue and relation, upheld an ideal of human potential through faith.

The Psychology of Help

How do our ideals of relation and community, if not faith, extend to the manner in which we treat each other? Is the function of help inherent to human beings? In the opening session of the "psychology of help" meetings that began in October 1944 and concluded in March 1945, Erich Fromm proposed that "helping" was, in fact, "the most basic human function that exists."[47] Further, Fromm stated, "One might think of the fact that [men] need relatedness to others as a matter of existence, that they cannot live without the help that they derive from the very presence of another human being."[48] He believed that the act of helping was a basic component of being human and implied a level of ethical relatedness to one's fellow human being. But Fromm also believed this basic human quality was being culturally negated. His strong stance pertaining to the power of the social order shifted somewhat during the final years the NYPG met. Fromm believed that "our culture so far has been far away from the idea of human help as part of the normal social process."[49] Again, witnessing the very real breakdown of societies in Europe affected what members discussed and how subjects were categorized. A schism developed between what was perceived (if not hoped) to be a human being's essential nature and the collapse of social and cultural structures that were blamed for not fostering these innate traits for just fellowship and relationship.

Fromm's opening statements at this first meeting on the psychology of help are quite fascinating. The group's discussions had clearly made

46 NYPG, 20 May 1942.

47 NYPG, 20 October 1944.

48 Ibid.

49 Ibid.

shifts throughout the years. During the final year, psychological problems and psychological help were seen as increasingly ambiguous. Indeed, a confidence in the ability of psychological help, so prevalent in the first years the group met, became less of a contrast to religious help in the final year of meetings. Discussions during the final year placed psychology and theology as companions in the task of facilitating human health and development. In a surprising foreshadow to the main thrust of Viktor Frankl's and other existential psychotherapeutic philosophies, Fromm stated, "People want help in making sense of one's own existence.... [T]oday there is an enormous amount of bewilderment.... [M]uch of the psychic help which people need today is that of finding some philosophical, religious or ethical orientation as to what sense life makes."[50] Fromm then states the inherent philosophical presuppositions psychology tends to ignore: "One of the questions we might discuss, then, is to what extent the psychic helper has the function in our culture of helping people to find some philosophical orientation. Today it seems as if psychiatrists have taken up the task of priests and other such helpers. The philosophy they stand for, as a rule, is as metaphysical or religious as any theologian could have."[51]

These surprising statements set the tone for the final meetings that followed. The seeking of help and the giving of help were seen as inherent human qualities. So what kind of help did people really want? Were people seeking a new authority or new direction? Do we naturally seek advice? Who dispenses advice, and do we expect particular people in our culture to be bestowed with wisdom, perspective, experience, and objectivity? Ultimately, do human beings need "reliable human contact"[52] in order for healthy and positive development to occur? And what constitutes reliable? As Alfried Längle would state decades later, we are essentially "dialogical" beings: Our existence is not only contingent upon dialogue and relation with others but dialogue, contact, and, by extension, reliable and dependable interaction, culminates in meaningful and positive growth and development.

---

[50] Ibid.

[51] Ibid.

[52] Erich Fromm, NYPG, 20 October 1944.

Again, seen within the context and backdrop of catastrophic world events, each human being, the NYPG argued, faced confusion about his or her identity and capabilities. What might emerge to restore solidarity and a genuine capacity to care for and aid another human being? Who was reliable, who possessed wisdom in what Fromm described as a bewildering age? Outlining several key questions for the group to discuss, Fromm foreshadows much of postmodern critical psychology. First, were there philosophical, religious, or political differences that placed limitations on psychology's generalizations about help? What kind of person was capable of dispensing psychological help? Was there a difference if the analysand believed in God but the analyst did not? What was implicit and explicit about the goals of therapy? In addition, should implicit and explicit philosophical positions be examined in the various psychological approaches? And, finally, what was the aim of psychological help, and was there a uniform criterion for health? "Is the aim of help," Fromm asked, "adjustment to society or is it the maximum realization of individual potentialities"?[53] Fromm thought that psychology had not come close to examining these issues and yet they were becoming increasingly pertinent.

Themes of solidarity, security, and psychology's ultimate mandate abounded in the last year the NYPG met. These three loose themes emerged out of discussions on psychological help. Helping another human being assumed ethics of goodwill and solidarity. Both psychology and the church equally were criticized by members of the NYPG for failing to provide a sense of solidarity or an ethic about what binds us together. Psychology was criticized for its promotion of the idea of "security" and its attachment to psychological health. Security implied an attainable, stable, and universal standard of psychological health. Increasingly, however, members spoke of the ambiguity of human life and the near impossibility of fully understanding what made us truly human: Were we really secure, and was security something we could honestly obtain and experience as stable? Harry Bone commented during a meeting in 1944 that life was both precarious and stable. There was, in fact, no absolute security for human values.[54] During the 12 January 1945 meeting, Erich Fromm declared, "The word security has become almost a fetish of modern

[53] Ibid.

[54] NYPG, 10 November 1944.

psychological thinking.... How can anyone be secure in view of the cosmic forces, and living in such a world as ours and in light of history"?[55] Fromm's statement evoked the sentiment and experience shared by all members during these years.

The conversation then turned to psychology's objective. Was psychology's objective really adjustment to society? If this were so, could psychology honestly claim it did not play a part in social ethics or an individual's responsibility regarding the social world? Harry Bone suggested that therapy represented an arena in which "unfulfilled potentialities [will] have an opportunity to begin their realization."[56] But did psychology direct those potentialities toward an adjustment to society or did psychology limit itself to the potentialities of the individual without context? When would therapy be successfully concluded, Bone asked, and he wondered whether "a better adjustment to society" was an appropriate indication.[57] Underneath these statements was the degree to which the psychologist or minister was an authority in determining the criteria for adjustment and whether an individual was so adjusted. The assumption by most psychologists in the group, not surprisingly, was that the minister could not be an objective authority and was, as a result, incapable of making such an evaluation. The minister, it was maintained, would necessarily bring his own theology to bear, and this, both Harrison Elliott and Carl Rogers agreed, was where the counseling process stopped and why the minister should not engage in therapy. However, psychology itself could not claim it was making value-neutral judgments, and this would extend to any theoretical pronouncements on what constituted a healthy adjustment (or not) to society. Indeed, this limitation raised the ever-present and thorny issue of the value judgments present in the act of helping, the division of authority in helping, and what kind of values were either being upheld or abandoned. This issue was further compounded by whether one could claim that the social world was stable and that adjustment to it was the key to mental health. Psychology claimed to be value-neutral, and yet psychological help was seen in many ways as an engagement in the ethics of social adjustment. On some level, psychologists

[55] NYPG, 12 January 1945

[56] NYPG, 10 November 1944.

[57] Ibid.

were engaged in coordinating individual potentialities and responsibilities with the demands of the social world. Directing his comments to the psychologists, Tillich stated, "Would you allow a human being to say to [himself] 'I am what I am; everything that I have done or that I have omitted is by necessity so'? Would this not mean that [he] accepts [himself] in totality, past and present, which means that [he] does not need to say 'I could have done better; I should have done differently.'"[58] Tillich continued, "Do we look at our being as a whole, as a totality of processes or as a complex entity of decisions in which we are responsible [rather than] events which drive us."[59]

In the final meetings of the NYPG, questions and debates continued about psychology's objectivity and whether the therapist's role was one of social adjustment. Also considered was the link between psychological health and development and the individual's freedom to challenge him- or herself and ask profoundly whether he or she could have "done better," as Tillich posited. In his 12 January 1945 presentation, theologian David E. Roberts challenged the psychologists present, "Surely your own worldview will operate consciously or unconsciously as a guiding criterion in estimating the extent to which the other person is facing reality or evading it."[60] Roberts added, "Therapy has often been represented as more presuppositionless than it actually is."[61] "In trying to form an appraisal of therapy," he continued, "I am troubled by certain antinomies. The paradox of promoting human autonomy and responsibility from within the context of complete determinism seems to me to be no more puzzling, but also no less puzzling, than the traditional theological dispute about free will and predestination."[62] Psychologists in the group, however, continued to uphold the ideals of scientific objectivity by claiming that the therapist, rather than the minister, was able to exercise restraint in terms of influencing therapy with value judgments. Yet Roberts made the astute observation that psychology, in fact, upheld strong values of self-sufficiency and autonomy, and he then asked whether these psychological ideals should be upheld over and above ideals of solidarity, community, and

[58] NYPG, 10 November 1944.

[59] Ibid.

[60] NYPG, 12 January 1945.

[61] Ibid.

[62] Ibid.

responsibility to others. Again, preceding much debate in the decades to follow about the extent to which psychology was stripped of social responsibility, Roberts stated, "From some Christian standpoints at least, the psychotherapeutic attempt to achieve a certain kind of autonomy or self-sufficiency is subject to the perils of self-deception and escapism."[63] Roberts also wanted clarification on "how to tell where resistance to society is healthy or neurotic and where adjustment to society is healthy or neurotic."[64] Who would decide this and how could the criteria for such decisions be value-free?

This rekindled the debate as to whether the promotion of individual dignity and uniqueness, in addition to autonomy and empowerment, was really the polar opposite of community and solidarity. Did psychology even attempt to integrate these issues? Dr. Grace Elliott offered a reflective critique of her own discipline when she presented to the group on 9 February 1945. Psychological help, Elliott contended, aimed at "achieving community in relationship with [his] fellows, or social solidarity."[65] Elliott saw an urgent need for community. The "infantile solidarity of totalitarianism," she maintained, "must move towards mature solidarity."[66] Critiquing psychology's lack of attention to this issue, Elliott stated, "Without specific provision for this need much of the individually oriented help given to individuals becomes ineffectual."[67] Elliott renewed the idea that psychological help and what constituted "adjustment" was often a precarious balance of fostering individual potential in light of that individual being simultaneously a social being, inextricably linked to the social world. Stating that there "can be no perfect person, scheme, theory or plan,"[68] Elliott foreshadows what Viktor Frankl and Alfried Längle strongly advocated in the decades to come; that is, that "[man] needs a set of values, a sense of direction, a frame of reference for [his] life."[69] But was this psychology's mandate, and were these the foundations of help?

---

[63] Ibid.
[64] Ibid.
[65] NYPG, 9 February 1945.
[66] Ibid.
[67] Ibid.
[68] Ibid.
[69] Grace Elliott, NYPG, 9 February 1945.

If we needed these things, we also were seen as increasingly demanding them from people perceived to be authorities of help. What difficulties did a minister, for example, face in pastoral counseling? Otis Rice offered an interesting picture of the complex issues that he confronted in a paper he gave to the group in December 1944 (interestingly, the psychologists in the group did not reflect on their own roles when presumably they were confronted with a similar array of complex issues). Rice stated,

> The apparent problems or needs presented vary greatly. There are simple questions of fact. There are other problems that appear as specifically theological, purely as matters of faith. Others seem as obviously matters of emotional conflict or of personal, social or vocational procedure.... With the great variety in type and severity of the needs in mind, I believe my first concern is to determine whether I may safely or productively undertake to help the individuals who come to me. One danger for the parish priest is [his] propensity for acquiring a beltful of spiritual scalps under the guise of 'saving souls'.... In a sense, then, from the beginning of the contact I am forced to make a tentative appraisal of the situation and a very rough and very provisional interpretation of what I believe to be the real meaning of the problem no matter in what form it is presented or disguised. I must try to make clear that this is no 'snap judgment' nor in any manner of speaking a 'diagnosis.' I attempt to listen intelligently enough so as to learn what the parishioner is saying and feeling, yet at the same time being alert to the 'danger signals' of situations with which I know I am not competent to deal.[70]

Rice's honest appraisal of help generated what could be called jurisdictional debates over exactly who had authority to deal with particular problems. This not only raised the question of categorizing "problems," but also of categorizing and separating the people who could deal effectively with some issues and not with others. Who was qualified to help whom? Who, in society, was perceived to have greater authority in helping? Interestingly, theologian Seward Hiltner believed the medical doctor possessed the greatest authoritarian role, whereas Erich Fromm believed the priest had a greater social authority.

Aside from who had authority, the issue of transmitting values also became key once again. It was assumed that the priest or minister would be

---

[70] NYPG, 8 December 1944.

conveying religious values in any kind of therapeutic intervention. Fromm argued that the priest or minister was bound by a set of philosophical and theological convictions. It was also assumed that these convictions would, in fact, limit the extent to which a parish priest or minister could effectively "help" a parishioner. As Fromm sarcastically commented, "How far is the conflict of a person to be looked upon from philosophical angles?"[71]

Tillich acknowledged the inherent values a minister or priest would pass on. He suggested, however, that psychology, if analyzed properly, could not be seen as being a value-less activity either. Harry Bone similarly queried whether there was "any content of moral values in the mind of the therapist either that he conveys to the client or whether he even uses it to guide his psychotherapeutic procedure."[72] Therapy or the counseling process would ideally, Bone argued, assist an individual in finding a personal view of life or frame of reference, and the "more completely free from value judgments the therapeutic procedure is, the more satisfactory it is."[73] Once again, was psychology value-free, or could it be? Tillich stated that in this "so-called value-less counseling the very fact that the value judgment is hidden is a crucial point."[74] Carl Rogers ended the December meeting by suggesting that counselors do hold value judgments: "It is only that [he] restrains [himself] in a situation where [he] wants to promote psychological growth."[75] Again, we are faced with the thorny issue of whether this implies the theologian or pastoral counselor is incapable of restraining value judgments, and if so, would this inhibit the process and outcome of therapeutic help, and by extension, positive psychological growth. Could or should ministers do therapy? By the same token, to what extent is psychology actually value-free, and what does "restraint" on the part of the therapist actually mean when placed up against a concept of help? What is psychological help, then? As we will see in Alfried Längle's theory of Existential Analysis, psychological growth and development, indeed psychological "help," is contingent upon the open spontaneous dialogue discovered in an I/thou encounter.

---

[71] NYPG, 8 December 1944.
[72] NYPG, 8 December 1944.
[73] Ibid.
[74] NYPG, 8 December 1944.
[75] NYPG, 8 December 1944.

To this end, David E. Roberts outlined several problems ministers faced in terms of how they were perceived by the public and what was expected of them. The minister, Roberts stated, was "supposed to be kindly, interested in people, generous and sympathetic; [he] is available without payment of special fees, to almost anyone who seeks [his] help.... The minister is expected to believe in the possibility of salvaging shattered human lives; [he] represents the converting power of religion."[76] Except for the transmission of fees, much of this description would fit the role of therapist. Therapists themselves believe in the transforming possibilities, if not converting power, of psychology. Roberts believed that ministers were restricted by a prescribed "set of answers"; rather than "assisting the individual to develop capacities for self-help through maturing emotionally,"[77] ministers, according to Roberts, more often presented a set of answers.

> [These answers] consist largely of generalizations about sin, salvation, God, Christ, the Bible, the Church, immortality, social progress, sex mores, and the omnipotence of faith, hope and love. All too often these "answers" do not contain much of the minister's own spontaneous feelings, reactions and reflections. They are built up largely in terms of what his denominational standards demand and what is appealing to his congregation.[78]

Roberts's comments are quite interesting. Superimposing some of the recent debate in critical psychology, for example, psychology has been questioned about the theoretical generalizations it relies upon and, in turn, perpetuates in therapy through the answers a therapist may provide. Even if the therapist subscribes to a therapeutic model and does his or her best not to impose answers on the clients, therapists are still confronted by clients who may (and often do) expect answers from psychology, if not, at the very least, some input from the therapist. To what extent does psychology meet the demands and expectations of its "congregation"?

The assumption Roberts leaves us with is that a minister may impede the ideal of psychological growth through the imposition of religious responses. Rather than facilitating an individual's own inner resources,

---

[76] NYPG, 12 January 1945.

[77] Ibid.

[78] Ibid.

strengths, and "answers," ministers respond to the questions brought forth by parishioners with fixed answers under the assumption that these answers will provide the necessary help. This ideal, however, seems just that. And it seems nearly impossible to suggest that psychology itself doesn't meet the needs of its "congregation" with theoretical generalizations or that it imposes values or diagnoses that may or may not hinder the process of developing a client's own inner resources.

Another very interesting point Roberts raised is the difference in responsibility between the therapist and minister. Roberts suggests that the minister is in many ways expected to be "a watch dog of conventional morality."[79] As Roberts states:

> It is often difficult for a minister to take a permissive attitude toward some forms of unconventional behavior.... [He] has to recognize that [he] has a responsibility to whole families and to a whole parish.... The therapist, on the other hand, is responsible solely to [his] client; and within very broad limits [he] can let conventions go hang for the sake of getting to the bottom of the trouble.[80]

What is fascinating about these comments is the degree to which the therapeutic process itself and the individuals within therapy are stripped of responsibility. Do therapists, for example, really have a limited amount of responsibility toward their clients and the issues clients bring to therapy? Roberts's comments suggest that even in the mid-1940s, psychology was perceived as having limited social responsibility and that a division between the individual and the social, rather than the two being inextricably linked, was clearly entrenched. Expanding psychology's responsibility was taken up quite vocally by Viktor Frankl and many other existential and humanistically oriented psychologists in the decades to come.

In the final year the NYPG met, theologians were very vocal about not only the limitations of psychology, but also the limitations and difficulty of conducting therapy from a ministerial context. Theologians within the group were eager to share and discuss what was becoming a growing demand on them; that is, dealing with issues brought to them by members of their congregations that were not necessarily religious in nature.

---

[79] Ibid.

[80] Ibid.

Although differences abounded between psychologists and theologians about individual and social responsibility and the imposition of values when helping fellow human beings, both sides reflected the growing ambiguity and uncertainty of analyzing human nature.

Conclusion

In a paper given to the group in 1943, Paul Tillich described the "eccentricity of the human mind," which made it impossible to formulate what he called a "closed system" in relation to being. Clearly taking aim at the dependence on science and the claims of theoretical certainty that the discipline of psychology was increasingly adopting, Tillich was suggesting how ambiguous human nature was and the near impossibility of capturing what it is that makes a human being truly human. To accept this ambiguity, David E. Roberts felt that psychology had to take a position on what he called mankind's "metaphysical and religious hunger."[81] To do this, psychology could not isolate itself from philosophical or theological considerations, all of which gained from each other and were what bound us together.[82]

The minutes and paper presentations of the New York Psychology Group offer a fascinating illustration of the attempt to bind psychological, philosophical, and theological concerns. Despite differences of opinion and disciplinary or vocational biases, members of the NYPG fielded challenging and honest questions about the limitations of both psychology and theology. The flood of questions raised by the group shows how ambiguous large issues such as faith, health, and care were considered, as highlighted within these interdisciplinary discussions, and there was little attempt to formulate clear and distinctive answers. What the group did share was a profound concern for the world and its inhabitants. In the chapters that follow, many of the same questions and concerns about psychology and, more generally, our ability to take seriously the human need for value and meaning will continue to be raised in interdisciplinary dialogue between theology and psychology and within psychology alone.

---

[81] NYPG, 12 January 1945.

[82] David E. Roberts, NYPG, 12 January 1945.

3

The Meaning of My Existence and the Responsibility for Our Existence: Viktor E. Frankl's Existential Challenge to Psychology

> If the concept of a will to meaning is idealistic at all, I would call such idealism the real realism. If we are to bring out the human potential at its best, we must first believe in its existence and presence. Otherwise man too will "drift"; he will deteriorate. For there is a human potential at its worst as well! And in spite of our belief in the potential humanness of man we must not close our eyes to the fact that *humane* humans are, and probably will always remain, a minority. But it is precisely for this reason that each of us is challenged to *join* the minority. Things are bad. But unless we do our best to improve them, everything will become worse.[1]

An Emerging Psychology of Responsibility

Is it idealistic to state that we must believe in and should strive for such things as love, community, responsibility, care for self and others, and social justice? How do beliefs in human potential relate to psychological health? Should psychologists convey such beliefs, actively instill hope and responsible, caring behavior to their clients? Is this part of psychology's mandate? The quotation that begins this chapter is taken from Viktor Frankl's book *The Unconscious God.* Originally a lecture given to a Viennese audience in 1947, the quote reflects the ethical appeal that Frankl had begun directing toward psychology as early as the 1930s and which characterized much of his writing following his release from Auschwitz in 1945. In the shadow of psychology's growing cultural influence, amidst

---

[1] Viktor E. Frankl, *The Unconscious God* (New York: Washington Square Press, 1985) 84.

the context and aftermath of WWII, the burgeoning Cold War, and the proliferation of nuclear weapons, Frankl's appeal for humane and responsible action extended to the discipline of psychology. When Frankl began his first lecture tour in the United States in 1957, audiences were introduced to a theoretical and therapeutic approach that linked the meaning and value of human existence with individual psychological health and development.

This chapter explores Frankl's challenge to psychology during this period as he began reaching an English audience through the publication of *The Doctor and the Soul* in 1955 and the series of six lectures he gave at Harvard Divinity School in 1957. Frankl's challenge, itself a product of historical, social, and political events, was embedded in his theory of Logotherapy. That challenge not only advocated an active ethical and social role for the psychologist, it stressed the importance of expanding psychology's vision of human nature. An expanded vision included the multiple meanings and values, both individual and cultural, which influenced the experiences we had of ourselves and our perceptions of well-being. Further, Frankl introduced the important therapeutic role responsibility played, again both individually and collectively, in psychological well-being and development.

The examples drawn from Frankl's body of work for this chapter illustrate yet another exploration and dialogue undertaken between psychology and religion during the mid-twentieth century. Within Frankl's message and theory, attention focuses on many themes that also had dominated the discussions of the NYPG.[2] These include a tone of urgency about the state of the world and, more specifically, the mental and spiritual health of individual citizens, the idea that interdisciplinary discussion and action was necessary to literally bring people together as opposed to further isolating them, and a questioning of psychology's mandate and purpose. What was seen as problematic about psychology? Why should psychology's mandate be broadened, and how did a dialogue between religion and psychology help in this endeavor? Did psychology have a responsibility beyond the individual, and what was a therapist's responsibility? Was psychology generally, and therapists specifically,

---

[2] The New York Psychology Group of the National Council on Religion and Higher Education, 1941–1945, hereafter cited as NYPG. From the collection of Prof. Allison Stokes of Ithaca College, New York.

responsible for facilitating the creation of the "good" citizen? Once again, familiar themes, yet themes that characterized the lectures and meetings during Frankl's initial foray into North American universities.

The intellectual climate and interdisciplinary dialogue going on between theology and psychology in the United States during the mid-twentieth century made Frankl's first visit in 1957 both timely and opportune. Frankl's challenge to the discipline of psychology was met by a receptive audience in the late 1950s at many theological seminaries in the United States. Many theologians had, since the 1930s, found dialogue between theology and psychology both fruitful and necessary. The previous chapter focused on the discussions between theologians and psychologists during the meetings of the New York Psychology Group from 1941 to 1945. Psychology's place and function within culture and theology's response to, and integration of, psychological theory and practice continue in the next chapter with a focus on Hans Hofmann's direction of the Harvard Project on Religion and Mental Health in the late 1950s. Further, in the late 1950s and early 1960s, the Academy of Religion and Mental Health continued to bring theologians and psychologists together at its yearly symposiums. The symposiums of the ARMH covered such topics as moral values in psychoanalysis and dialogues between religion, culture, science, and mental health. All of these examples are a testament to the rich dialogue that took place in the mid-twentieth century.

Frankl's first trip to the United States was sponsored by the Religion in Education Foundation. His nationwide tour included a series of six lectures at Harvard Divinity School in September 1957. The audiences of these lectures represented a diverse mix of psychologists, medical faculty, and theologians, many of whom would continue to cross paths in the years to come. Harvard psychologist Gordon Allport, for example, would later play an important role in introducing Frankl's book *Man's Search for Meaning* to American publishers. Theologian Hans Hofmann of Harvard Divinity School, the moderator at one of Frankl's six lectures, would take up the position of director of the Harvard Project on Religion and Mental Health that same year. Frankl, Hofmann, and Paul Tillich also became involved in the Academy of Religion and Mental Health. One 1962 meeting of the ARMH, for example, advertised a luncheon lecture given by Frankl followed by a dinner lecture delivered by Tillich. Frankl and Tillich were also on the editorial board of the *Review of Existential Psychology and*

Psychiatry from 1961 to 1965. Articles by the two men appeared side by side in the first issue of the review in 1961.

Grace Cali, Tillich's secretary at Harvard, recalls Tillich being introduced to Frankl by Hans Hofmann. Although it is difficult to ascertain the exact dates the meeting between Tillich and Frankl took place, one could surmise that it occurred during Frankl's first lecture tour in 1957. According to Cali, Tillich had read Frankl's first English publication, *The Doctor and the Soul*, and found the concepts of Logotherapy "very compatible with his own ideas...although he admitted later to me he had some difficulty digesting the coined term of Logotherapy."[3] These associations and the many that followed were ones Frankl relied on and gained from in the years that followed.

Frankl embodied a particular philosophical position when he came to lecture in the United States. In the quotation that begins this chapter, he seemed to foreshadow the reception his theory would receive in the States for decades to come. Was it idealistic or realistic to suggest that psychologists might play an active social role in helping to facilitate a just and humane world? Frankl was calling on therapists and psychology as a whole to be directly involved in creating a better world, beginning with each individual and progressing outward. Was this psychology's role, though? Were there particular values of justice and compassion, for example, that psychological theory and practice should promote? As we will see in chapter 5, many postmodern critiques of psychology, particularly those within critical psychology, have decried the transmission of values in theory, and even more so within the therapeutic setting, as negative and highly problematic for psychology. In 1957, Frankl was not only stating that psychology did, in fact, transmit values (in other words, was not value-free), he suggested that some values were indeed worth upholding and transmitting.[4] But he argued that to do so effectively, psychology had to become increasingly aware of its own presuppositions, its foundational

---

[3] Grace Cali, *Paul Tillich First-Hand: A Memoir of the Harvard Years* (Chicago: Exploration Press, 1996) 68.

[4] What became problematic for Frankl was the continuous charge by critics that Logotherapy imposed values, and Judeo-Christian ones at that. Frankl's appeal that humanity must believe and maintain values of community, responsibility, peace, and justice, for example, was assumed by him to be values that all human beings understood and could bind us together universally.

philosophies, its intent, and what specific values it was, in fact, transmitting. Frankl was suggesting that psychology needed to become much more self-reflective in order to become more relevant.

In the years that followed, critics of Logotherapy would, however, continually charge that it imposed Judeo-Christian values and an overt message of social responsibility onto its clients.[5] Many felt that Frankl's theory of Logotherapy was not psychology but a derivative of religion or philosophy, and a weak one at that. The imposition of values, especially responsibility, was linked to the role of religion and not psychology. Further, Frankl's inclusion of religion, philosophy, politics, and ethics tended to marginalize Logotherapy within psychological circles. Frankl's theory continually struggled for legitimacy on the margins of what was deemed psychology "proper" because it was felt to lack empirical validity, and the interdisciplinary alliances he engaged in were deemed separate from psychology's mandate. Labeling Frankl's theory "quasi-religious beliefs,"[6] for example, was a common sentiment in North America during the 1960s and 1970s. Many articles written on Frankl's theory during these same decades debated what Logotherapy was and attempted to unearth its latent religious themes. Earl A. Grollman discussed what he called the jurisdictional problems between psychology and religion in an article on Frankl in 1964. Grollman felt that Frankl had "done much to enlarge the conversation between psychology and religion."[7] Indeed, by the time of Frankl's death in 1997, his approach to psychology, particularly therapy, was recategorized as "unique" and hailed as "re-humanizing medicine and psychotherapy."[8] Here we have an obvious example of psychology's own

[5] In a harsh review of Frankl's book *The Will to Meaning*, Bernard Steinzor characterizes the criticism Frankl received over the issue of values when he stated, "You [Frankl] characterize the values you share with your class and culture as universal and thus objective." Bernard Steinzor, "Thinking Meaningfully About Emptiness," *Psychiatry and Social Science Review* 3/9 (September 1969): 26.

[6] "Logotherapeutical Sermon," an anonymous British review of Frankl's *The Doctor and the Soul* (New York: Vintage Books, 1986) in *Psychiatry and Social Science Review* (2 June 1970): 17.

[7] Earl A. Grollman, "Viktor E. Frankl: A Bridge Between Psychiatry and Religion," *Conservative Judaism* 14/1 (Fall 1964): 20.

[8] A common and repeated expression used in the obituaries following Frankl's death in 1997.

precarious definitions and labels as to what constitutes psychological theory and practice.

Throughout this chapter, an attempt is made to illustrate Frankl's contribution to this rich dialogue in the late 1950s. Frankl, much like those involved in the NYPG, felt that the time had come to question seriously whether values such as justice, responsibility, compassion, and peace among human beings belonged solely within the realm of religion. Along with this questioning came a reevaluation of what was missing in psychology and psychology's place in our society.

However one feels about the theoretical structure of Logotherapy, by 1957 Frankl was calling for an explicit acknowledgment of the active and influential role that psychologists and psychological theory play in Western culture. If, as Frankl suggested, psychologists were witness to, and highly influential interpreters of, the human condition, did psychology stop there? Were they not also witnesses to the reality of our infinite potential and creativity? And did psychology stop there? Psychology, and therapists specifically, were also participants. Since therapists encountered individuals and participated in the intricate and intimate layers of being human, could psychology realistically claim to be a neutral and objective enterprise? If the transmission of values is inevitable, and given psychology's cultural stature, should psychology be influential in transmitting ethical responsibility and social justice? If a psychologist's role was characterized as aiding, assisting, and possibly healing a fellow human being—if psychologists on some level entered the profession with a fundamental concern for another person's well-being—then for the sake of humanity's continuation, development, and growth, such a role required a belief in, and embodiment of, our infinite potential. This, Frankl suggested, was not necessarily a negative thing. If psychology had both power and influence, what might it powerfully influence?

Frankl's position was, of course, influenced by his own experience with the events of WWII, his incarceration in several concentration camps over a two-and-a-half-year period, his professional position as both a neurologist and psychotherapist, his Jewish and European heritage, and the influence of mid-twentieth-century European intellectual thought, specifically existential philosophy. All of these contexts influenced his ethical, social, and political position and, in turn, influenced his theory. Is Logotherapy, then, too far from the parameters of psychology's mandate, or is it possible to see Frankl's theory specifically, and psychology potentially, as positive and active contributors to ethical existence generally? In a 1969 review of Frankl's book *The Will to Meaning*, Bernard Steinzor took aim at what he felt was Frankl's lack of social commentary. He stated, "Your [Frankl's] life was deeply affected by a social catastrophe, yet you hardly address any comments to the problems of communal action to seek justice in the struggle against authoritarianism, militarism, racism, poverty, and imperialism. Your index doesn't contain any reference to rage, violence, or hate, and you do not noticeably discuss evil and injustice."[9] While one can argue that Frankl's publications for large general audiences did not overtly tackle "communal action" or "discuss evil and injustice," his existential perspective always paired the paradoxical relationship between our human capacity for evil and injustice alongside our potential for creative good. Once again, the quotation that begins this chapter is indicative of Frankl's acknowledgment that human beings are capable of both good and evil. Further, the numerous lectures Frankl gave, particularly in the United States, often addressed social issues, and as we shall see later in this chapter, Frankl discussed the link between individual development and communal action in light of world events to his Harvard audience in 1957. Finally, much of Frankl's theory and writings embody his personal attitude toward life. His writings acknowledge the contradictions inherent in being human, but they convey a deep conviction that a positive approach to life is ultimately stronger and more creatively enduring.

We now look specifically at Frankl's first English publication in 1955 and the introduction of his theory of Logotherapy. To do this, we look at five specific points: the spiritual dimension, the will to meaning, self-transcendence, freedom, and responsibility.

The Doctor and the Soul

In 1955, Frankl's theory of Logotherapy was introduced to a new English audience with the publication of *The Doctor and the Soul* in the United States. The book was initially listed in the *New York Times* under the heading "recent religious books."[10] This classification of Frankl's first

---

[9] Grollman, "Bridge," 25.

[10] *The New York Times* (1857–Current File) 19 November 1955, 12; ProQuest Historical Newspapers *The New York Times*, "Recent Religious Books" section.

publication is a telling indication of the complex reception his work perpetually endured in North America until his death in 1997. The original manuscript, published in German in 1946 under the title *Ärztliche Seelsorge,*[11] had undergone a unique and profound journey. After branching out from studies in Freudian psychoanalysis and membership in Alfred Adler's Society for Individual Psychology, Frankl completed his first book-length manuscript on Logotherapy in the early 1940s while working as a neurologist and psychiatrist at a Viennese hospital. At the time of his deportation to the concentration camps in 1942, the manuscript remained with him tucked in the lining of his overcoat. As most of his belongings, including the clothes he wore, were confiscated as he entered his first camp, the manuscript was subsequently lost. Frankl carefully reconstructed this manuscript from memory, recording small notes during the duration of his two-and-a-half years in the camps. He later commented that the intellectual activity and challenge of reconstructing the manuscript saved him both mentally and spiritually.

The subtext throughout *The Doctor and the Soul* was the limitations of and prescription for (by way of a new theoretical perspective) psychology. Frankl had initially considered Logotherapy to be a supplement to established models of psychotherapy in an attempt to broaden the "concepts of man" that he believed anchored all psychological theory. As mentioned, we will look at five specific "supplements" Frankl introduced. These are the spiritual dimension, the will to meaning, self-transcendence, freedom, and responsibility. Each of the supplements overlaps throughout Frankl's work, depicting the complexity and creative nature of human existence.

---

[11] The English translation of the original German title of this book is "Medical Ministry." Frankl often used the term medical ministry to English audiences to describe Logotherapy. Although he was often ambiguous about any religious connotation, Frankl deliberately chose the original German title in order to "shock" the medical profession. The book was intended for medical doctors in order to convey the necessity and urgency of integrating a variety of perspectives with the medical model. Health required a multidimensional approach to heal the "whole" person. I wish to thank Dr. Alfried Längle of Vienna, Austria, who worked with Frankl for 10 years, for our many conversations over the past six years on this subject and his constant generosity in sharing these stories with me.

The Problem with Psychology

Frankl felt that the influence of science on psychological theory was detrimental to the discipline. What seemed increasingly problematic for psychology was the dependent use of scientific objectification to fuel psychological theory. A dependence on the seeming objectivity of scientific paradigms was based, in turn, on a belief and worldview that human phenomena could be analyzed in predictive and observable patterns of behavior and expression. Although Frankl was trained as a medical doctor and certainly did not object to the use of scientific paradigms, their increasing usage within psychology seemed out of step with what psychology did or what it was supposed to accomplish. From an existential foundation, Frankl sought to coordinate a multidimensional approach to psychological health and well-being. Wanting to address the "whole" human being, Frankl's Logotherapy was a mixture of psychological theory and practical therapeutic techniques embedded with medical, philosophical, religious, existential, and ethical perspectives.

The theoretical conceptualizations about human nature within the discipline of psychology, according to Frankl, had been "constrained by biological, psychological [and] by sociological factors."[12] For Frankl, human existence was marked by its inherent freedom. Human beings were deciding beings, capable of analyzing, contemplating, and putting into context the multiple structures and realities to which they belonged, by which they were influenced, and to which they could freely choose an attitude. We were free to decide whether these structures produced limitations, whether they were challenging and created possibility, whether they motivated us and offered potential to transcend, modify, or change these same structures. Human beings, according to Frankl, existed within "structured spaces" and historical existence.[13] While these multiple contexts influenced and could be internalized experientially as an individual's reality, these same "structured spaces" provided only partial glimpses into human existence. Psychology, in Frankl's opinion, had limited its analysis of human existence to these structured spaces, be they psychological,

---

[12] Frankl, *The Doctor and The Soul*, 20.

[13] Ibid., 26.

biological, or sociological, but had not adequately addressed the subjective experiential level. Neither had it attempted to probe a fundamental existential question: What made a human being truly human? The experiential level revealed how any one individual responds to, adopts an attitude toward, or makes decisions for or against these structured spaces. Without doubt, one can argue that these subjective experiences are embedded in these very structured spaces so that the line between what is clearly individual and what is collectively experienced is somewhat blurred. But for Frankl, psychology had subsumed that ambiguous subjective experiential level into theoretical generalizations. Psychological reality for Frankl, indeed psychological development and well-being, was discovered in the precarious and complex middle ground of both social and cultural context and subjective experience.

The Spiritual Dimension

Frankl expanded the established two-dimensional structure of the human psyche in Freudian and Jungian psychoanalysis to include a third spiritual dimension. The spiritual dimension represented the core of the human psyche. It embodied wholeness and the union of body, mind, and spirit. Each dimension, beginning with the somatic, permeated the next to depict ever-expanding and inclusive levels of human consciousness. The spiritual dimension represented the location of and source for what Frankl identified as truly human phenomena. Frankl expanded the existing theoretical model of the human psyche in order to account for those capacities, potentials, and experiences that defied strict definition under somatic and psychic theorizing. Psychology, Frankl believed, needed to be open to these fluid human experiences, and it therefore required a language and structure to discuss human experience that was essentially open-ended and ambiguous. Something had to account for our uniquely "human" potential for and expression of such things as creativity, hope, faith, belief, love, relatedness, justice, despair, destructiveness, hate, and cynicism. Although one can argue that it is difficult to clearly ascertain what constitutes uniquely human phenomena, Frankl's point was that human experience, subjectively and collectively formed, always had the potential to defy the parameters of theory, especially psychological theory.

Although quick to defend the spiritual dimension as a secular psychological category that facilitated discussion about our potential for and experience of such things as faith and belief, Frankl was never able to argue convincingly to psychological and pastoral counseling audiences in North America that the spiritual dimension did not have a religious connotation. Despite this, many psychologists, medical doctors, and pastoral counselors felt indebted to the concepts he introduced. Concepts such as the spiritual dimension and self-transcendence did, in fact, provide a contemporary, humane, more expansive, and philosophical view of human existence that many in the "helping" professions found useful within therapy, in their relationships with clients or patients, and in their approach to clients who expressed feelings and experiences of suffering, hopelessness, and meaninglessness. Frankl's perspective on human existence and language also gave therapists, pastoral counselors, and medical doctors a wider, more multidimensional framework to discuss fundamental existence questions with their clients and patients. Indeed, broaching these existential realities within therapy and being willing to accept the ambiguity and complexity of human existence within the therapeutic realm made dialogue (as opposed to an objective, interpretive, and prescriptive approach) between therapist and client a point of relatedness and connection that facilitated the "healing" aspect of therapy.

Human existence, Frankl observed from an existential lens, was finite and somewhat predictable; yet human potential was always infinite. The essence of being human, what made us truly human, was the middle ground between the reality of finite existence and infinite potential and possibility. Navigating this middle ground was key to positive or "healthy" psychological development and the nexus point for the discovery of meaning and value in our lives.

The Search for Meaning

The search for meaning(s)[14] or the will to meaning, according to Frankl, was our primary motivation, the active and deliberate search for meaning and value in our lives. The will to meaning was a continuous life-long motivation. According to Frankl, we discover meaning through the

[14] Frankl used the plural form "meanings" to denote the continuous meanings that are potentially discovered throughout the course of one's life. The plural form was not to be mistaken with a notion of ultimate meaning. Critics of Frankl often felt he was in fact making a direct link between the meanings we discover in our lives and an ultimate meaning.

actualization of three values: creative, experiential, and attitudinal. By participating, engaging with, and responding to others in our community and the world, we could potentially discover meaning(s) through our work or any concrete creative contribution. Meanings were also potentially discovered at the subjective experiential level through our active dialogue and engagement with the world and with others. It was through dialogue and relation with others in addition to being open and receptive to the world experientially that we could discover moments of meaning and value related to one's own existence, such as love, community, justice, or beauty. "The greatness of a life," Frankl stated, "can be measured by the greatness of a moment."[15] Our willingness to be open and receptive in experiencing the value and dignity of another human being opens up the potential for discovering the meaningfulness inherent in each life and each moment. Finally, our human ability to freely choose and decide is reflected in the attitudes we adopt toward ourselves, toward others, and toward any situation in which we find ourselves. Our human freedom not only enables us to adopt an attitude, but it also allows us to change the attitudes we adopt and hold. We are free to become conscious of our attitudes, to look at them objectively, and to decide if they hinder our development and our relationship with others or whether they facilitate greater depth of experience and understanding (of both ourselves and others). For Frankl, the attitude we are potentially capable of as human beings in the face of suffering or unalterable crisis is particularly poignant. An existential psychotherapy acknowledges that human existence is marked by experiences of both tragedy and joy. Despite this dichotomous reality, any situation holds the possibility or potential of unconditional meaningfulness through the attitude and approach we choose at a given moment.

One could say that Frankl's contribution to an analysis of human reality was acknowledging that our existence, development, and well-being resides between two poles: reality and potential, finitude and infinite possibility, certainty and uncertainty. Human existence is a continuous movement and search toward meaning, a continuous creation and re-creation of meaning and certainty, both real and possible. Being human also requires an acknowledgment of and abandonment to what is uncertain, ambiguous, and possibly unknowable, and this is equally true for both

[15] Frankl, *The Doctor and the Soul*, 44.

science and religion. Following Frankl's logic, neither a secular nor a religious worldview fully conquers the uncertainty of human existence. This was certainly true of psychology. The health and well-being of humanity generally and individuals specifically within therapy resided in humane acknowledgment, acceptance, and understanding of the ambiguous yet meaningful contours of human existence.

Freedom

There are, of course, predictive aspects of human life, and Frankl did not deny these. Human beings are finite biological beings. Our physical development unfolds in a somewhat predictable yet finite process. Psychologically and experientially, human beings develop and express themselves often predictably, a reflection of neurological development as well as shared cultures, values, and social norms. Although we are constrained to some degree by our biological finiteness and by our shared social or communal realities (Frankl's structured spaces), there exist degrees of ambiguity and possibility in all human endeavors that point to our inherent freedom. Frankl linked and grounded the existential philosophical idea of freedom with the reality that human beings suffer, that they experience and inflict tragedy and conflict. Once again, influenced by existential rationale, Frankl brought together the idea of infinite possibility inherent in individual freedom with the realities of suffering, tragedy, and death. Together, this expanded picture of human reality made life unconditionally meaningful. The possibility and freedom to experience one's life as meaningful and valuable could be discovered at every moment, even at times of unexpected and unavoidable suffering. An individual suffering from terminal cancer or illness, for example, was, in Frankl's opinion, capable of transcending the immediate experience of physical suffering through his or her freedom of attitude toward the situation. The onset of disease and its progress through the body has of course some predictive elements. Cultural and familial responses to disease and inevitable death also factor into the meaning and value of the experience for the individual. Without denying these elements or their effect upon the individual, Frankl asks us to consider that the same individual simultaneously has the freedom to respond, take a stand, and adopt a particular and unique attitude toward these experiences and realities. At every moment there is a space of possibility, and an individual has the freedom to fill that space with a unique and distinctive response or attitude. A personal stand or decision emerging from the experiential level in tandem with a moment or situation of unavoidable suffering or tragedy was the ultimate expression of human freedom. Freedom and meaning were expressed and discovered through an awareness of and confrontation with the tragic and joyous events and moments of life and not through the denial or suppression of one or the other. Despite the reality of social or cultural structures, our relational predisposition, and our finitude as biological beings, our ability or potential to experience and derive meaning from difficult situations constituted human freedom.

Self-Transcendence

The idea that existence is a process of becoming influences what health, healing, growth, and development mean from an existential perspective. The description of becoming as process is linked to the idea of transcendence: of expansion, growth, development, an active movement oriented outside and beyond oneself, a striving experientially and literally toward an external point of reference. Our human ability and freedom to transcend a given situation or moment, even through attitude alone, implies considerable fluidity between psychological health and "ill-health." The notion of self-transcendence was contingent upon an amalgamated vision and analysis of both internal subjective experience and the world (the larger contexts) to which one belonged and in which one was embedded. The concept also alluded to a Judeo-Christian vision of the continuous transformation of humankind.

To summarize, Logotherapy was not limited to the internal psychic processes of an individual. Frankl's theory attempted to expand and coordinate both internal and external realities. He saw psychology as problematic because of its limited ability to coordinate internal and external reality; its inability to accept the ambiguous reality of being human; its downplaying of experiential manifestations of possibility and potential; and, finally, its unwillingness to confront the implicit foundational philosophies, values, and conceptualizations of humankind that framed theory and therapy. These limitations constrained what Frankl felt was a uniquely human and spirited capacity for unlimited potential in the midst of and never separated from the "structured spaces" or external contexts to which we are bound. The limitations on human existence evoked a "fragmentary quality"[16] to life, but this, Frankl argued, did not take away from the meaningfulness and value that life potentially held at every moment. Actualizing, or bringing into concrete expression, the potential meaningfulness and value of life was, in fact, our moral responsibility.

Responsibility

Morality, according to Frankl, was an inherent human quality linked with responsive action. As a theory and therapy, Logotherapy's aim was to guide a client toward a greater consciousness of their responsibility. Frankl's application of the term was heavily influenced by the Jewish concept of responsibility for others and for community. The concept of responsibility further linked the individual to the community, and it made psychological health and development contingent upon a reciprocal and mutually influential dialogue with an ethical duty toward "other." "The uniqueness of the human personality," Frankl wrote, "finds its meaning entirely in its role in an integral whole."[17] Further, "the value and dignity of the individual is dependent upon the community. But if the community itself is to have meaning, it cannot dispense with the individuality of the individuals who make it up."[18]

What was our individual responsibility? According to Frankl, life continually presented us with questions and challenges. It was our duty and responsibility as human beings, as individuals, to become increasingly conscious of and responsive to these challenges. Our individual freedom was linked to a moral and ethical obligation to respond both to others and to community. From a Logotherapeutic perspective, my individual existence is grounded in an essential freedom. I possess the freedom to make a certain decision or adopt a particular attitude at a specific moment in light of a situation that confronts me and in light of the subjective experience and perceptions I have. My moral and ethical obligation as a human being is then to respond and act beyond my individual freedom, beyond my subjectivity and singularity. Again, human existence is seen in a relational yet dichotomous sense. My existence is unique and yet my existence is grounded in relation and otherness. I am free, and yet my

[16] Frankl, *The Doctor and the Soul*, 66.
[17] Ibid., 70.
[18] Ibid., 71.

freedom is matched with an equal ethical obligation to respond and care for others.

Frankl's concept of responsibility is also linked to a fundamental belief in life's unconditional meaningfulness in spite of its finite and transitory character. Frankl defined responsibility as a response-in-action. Once again, the uniqueness and dignity of individual life and experience is upheld but seen in simultaneous dialogue with the external world. Our social embeddedness provided both freedom and restriction on our development and expression. Frankl's two-fold vision of humankind, freedom despite finitude, extended to his commentary on social behavior. Ethical behavior fell under this vision as well. Ethical behavior encompassed what was good for the community and what was of highest value to the individual. This two-fold view of existence preserved the uniqueness, value, and meaningfulness of individual life and experience but embedded that uniqueness in the reality of social responsibility and ethical acts that benefited the greater community. What was of value or what was deemed worthwhile behavior did not have to benefit the community.

> [There are] whole areas which are the private preserve of the individual. These are values which can or must be actualized aside from and independent of all community...the rich store of values which experiences with art or nature offer to the individual even in utter solitude is essentially and fundamentally personal; these values are valid whether or not the community profits from them. In saying this we are well aware that on the other hand there are a number of experiential values which by their nature are reserved to community experience. These may rest upon a broader basis (comradeship, solidarity, etc.).[19]

An Ethical Mandate for Psychology

This leads to our final point that distinguished *The Doctor and the Soul.* While Logotherapy challenged the mandate, foundational assumptions, and aims of psychology, Frankl was overt in introducing a moral and ethical mandate for psychology. Psychology, specifically Logotherapy, had a duty to convey a "positive" philosophy to its clients. Frankl criticized the rise and increasing categorization of psychological

---

[19] Ibid., 92.

problems such as "neurosis" and "syndromes." As we shall see in the following section, Frankl asked his Harvard audience in 1957 if we can scientifically account for the supposed increase in neurosis, possibly suggesting that psychology constructs psychological problems as much as it observes them. Psychology had to acknowledge its own presuppositions and perhaps be actively engaged in producing a more responsible citizenry. Frankl's answer is not without its problems either. How do you convey this to clients, and should you? While Frankl admits that Logotherapy resides on the "borderland" between medicine and religion, he clearly links psychological health and development to an ethical framework of responsibility and feels that psychologists or therapists have an ethical duty to convey guideposts for psychic health and development that merge precariously with specific social action and responsibility.

On the one hand, Logotherapy can be seen strictly in the context of Frankl's intent, as a supplement to established models of psychotherapy, another lens for broadening the analysis of human existence. At the same time, though, Frankl's overt ethical call and dialogue with religion raises even more questions about what psychology is, the role of therapists, and the near impossibility of claiming that psychology is an objective and neutral enterprise. Critics have often charged that Frankl's work lacks intellectual depth and substance. Despite these charges, Frankl's work, and particularly the two mid-twentieth century examples in this chapter, reveal a vocal and humane appeal that he felt belonged squarely within the domain and mandate of psychological theory and therapy. How are we to live peacefully and justly with each other? How can each of us reach our unique potential and also reach out and be concerned about our fellow human beings? This enormous appeal was made to two fairly powerful and influential voices within our culture: psychology and religion.

The Harvard Lectures: 1957

Frankl's ethical appeal, directed to the discipline of psychology and as social commentary, continued during his first lecture tour in the United States in 1957. In the spirit of dialogue and cooperation amongst psychologists and theologians, Frankl was invited to give a series of six lectures at Harvard Divinity School. Addressing an audience receptive to and active in what were perceived to be pressing social issues, Frankl outlined, once again, what was problematic about psychology. First, psychology had neglected the extent to which culture had impacted its own theoretical paradigms, despite the growing influence these same paradigms had on the wider culture. Second, psychology tended to restrict its analysis of human nature to individual intrapsychic processes. Even more problematic was psychology's fundamental belief that these individual processes could be analyzed apart from social context. For psychology to analyze human nature realistically, it was imperative, Frankl argued, for psychology to have an ear to society and culture. Third, psychology was anything but an ahistorical, apolitical enterprise. It was, rather, historically, culturally, politically, economically, ethically, and religiously interconnected. Our notions of psychological health and well-being, therefore, had to be seen, analyzed, and interpreted from a much wider interdisciplinary lens. In doing so, psychology needed not only to broaden the scope of its mandate, but also be aware of the foundational philosophies and values that contributed to its theoretical conceptions of what well-being and health meant. Whether stated implicitly or explicitly (generally implicitly), these foundational presuppositions influenced the images and concepts of human existence that, in turn, shaped and defined theory, research, and therapy.

Frankl's first lecture tour of the United States took place at a very interesting time. The intellectual climate and dialogue between existential and humanistic-oriented psychologists and theologians had preceded Frankl's arrival in the United States by several decades. Frankl's invitation, in the context of these ongoing dialogues, seems appropriate and timely. No doubt the classification of *The Doctor and the Soul* in *The New York Times* in 1955 under "new books in religion," the Religion in Education Foundation's sponsorship and organization of the tour, in addition to Frankl's own interdisciplinary style and approach to psychology contributed to the warm welcome he received at Harvard Divinity School.[20]

[20] Much of the material for this section is based on the six original audiotapes (reels 1–6) of these Harvard lectures and a typed manuscript of what is called the "master lecture" (Viktor Frankl, 21–27 September 1957, Graduate Theological Union Archives, Flora Lawson Hewitt Library, Graduate Theological Union, Berkeley CA). The Graduate Theological Union very generously allowed me to have the original audiotapes of the lectures transferred to CD. The quality of the original audiotapes is quite poor, compounded by Frankl's struggle with the English language. Because of these issues, I have not quoted extensively from this material. I would like to thank the GTU archives in Berkeley, California, for granting me access to these audiotapes,

Indeed these factors are telling indications as to where Frankl's theory made initial inroads in the United States: on the religious side of the psychology/religion divide. Frankl's own ambiguity about religion and the mixed reactions his theory and writings received meant that it was never clear whether his theory of Logotherapy fit the criteria of a strictly psychological model or whether it should be classified a "religious psychology." The varying responses to Frankl's work, as previously mentioned, illuminate several perpetual problems. And, once again, we see similar questions to those raised by members of the New York Psychology Group. First, what constitutes a psychological theory? Second, what images and theoretical positions about human nature are clearly psychological? Are there distinguishable boundaries around psychological theory and research that clearly demarcate psychological questions from religious about human nature and human development? Because of this complexity, one that seems to continue to this day, it seems fitting to look closely at the Harvard lectures.

The series of six lectures Frankl gave provides an excellent illustration of psychologists and theologians grappling with the possible dialogue, potential overlaps, and ambiguous demarcations between psychology and religion. The lectures are also an important illustration of the many dialogues going on mid-twentieth century about the limitations of psychology and psychology's ultimate role in society. These dialogues also have a very strong ethical appeal. The appeal made by both psychologists and theologians in 1957 entailed peaceful coexistence, love, knowledge of self and other, community, and, finally, individual and global responsibility. The appeal reacted to world and cultural events, and it proposed action in light of these events. The experiences of an increasingly capitalistic and technically fueled society, WWII, the Cold War, and the proliferation of nuclear weapons, for example, created a sense of humanitarian urgency for many. Psychology and theology equally were criticized for their neglect in addressing the ramifications of these social and historical events. Believing there to be a significant rise in mental and spiritual distress, psychologists and theologians came together to address major contemporary problems. Their proposed action was interdisciplinary

---

which are currently housed under the Viktor Frankl Library and Memorabilia at GTU.

dialogue, critical analysis, and frank questioning of the images of human existence that psychology was so influential in constructing and perpetuating. Further, more instructive ways to educate seminary students to deal with the lives and experiences of their twentieth century parishioners was also considered. Note that a more extensive integration of psychological curriculum in seminary schools became a major focus of the Harvard Project on Religion and Mental Health, for example.

Many theologians had been influenced by psychological theory. Its integration into the work of ministers was seen as a positive step forward, and yet many also joined a chorus of humanistic and existentially oriented psychologists who began questioning the narrowness of psychology. Erich Fromm had described psychology's mandate as ultimately manipulating and, therefore, negative. Psychology was seen as problematic because of its dependence on empirical objective science to theorize, categorize, and prescribe appropriate ways of being in the world that were further couched in the language of mental health, but "appropriate," Fromm believed, for the functioning of a capitalistic society and not necessarily for the enhancement of human potential.

The perspectives that contributed to the mid-twentieth century dialogue between psychologists and theologians held that human beings ultimately could not be known and could not be projected, thereby reduced, onto the plane of scientific or economic determinism. The assumption that psychology could ultimately "know" what it was to be human meant denying the possibility and potential for radical change, either at the individual or social level. Psychology's mandate of mental health was seen, ironically, as contributing to a process of alienation and isolation among individuals. In contrast, the existential perspectives and ethical appeal so prevalent in these mid-century dialogues saw mental health and psychological healing situated in the reconciliation, relationship, and union of self and other. At the time of Frankl's arrival in the United States, those engaged in an analysis of psychology's cultural role clearly felt that psychology could make significant contributions to the positive development not only of individuals, but also of a renewed, expanded, and more humble "concept of man," as Frankl often stated. But to do so, it needed society. The idea that human existence was ambiguous and ultimately unknowable would mean confronting the reality of human creativity, possibility, and potential as well as our restrictive capacities for destruction and hate. Erich Fromm provides an astute summary of the sentiment felt at the time:

> Modern [man] experiences [himself] as a *thing*, as an embodiment of energies to be invested profitably on the market. [He] experiences [his] fellow [man] as a thing to be used for profitable exchange. Contemporary psychology, psychiatry and psychoanalysis are involved in this universal process of alienation. The patient is considered as a thing, as the sum of many parts. Some of these parts are defective and need to be fixed. There is a defect here and a defect there, called symptoms, and the psychiatrist considers it his function to fix these various defects. [He] does not look at the patient as a global, unique whole, which can be fully understood only in the act of full relatedness and empathy.... [I]f psychoanalysis is to develop in this direction it has still unexhausted possibilities for human transformation and spiritual change. If it remains enmeshed in the socially patterned defect of alienation it may remedy this or that individual defect, but it will become another tool for making [man] more automatized, and adjusted to an alienated society.[21]

It is within this particular context of dialogue and sense of social urgency that Frankl began his first lectures in 1957 before a mixed audience of psychologists, psychiatrists, and theologians at Harvard Divinity School. Those who had read Frankl's book *The Doctor and the Soul* or were hearing him for the first time must have sensed the struggle he would encounter with his theory of Logotherapy in the United States. Hans Hofmann aptly remarked as moderator at one of Frankl's lectures, "We are here not only to be enchanted and delighted [by Dr. Frankl] but to help you [Frankl] face the American scene, the most raucous [no doubt will be] the psychoanalytic schools."[22]

Although Frankl was adept and comfortable speaking and writing in an interdisciplinary fashion, he had a somewhat complicated relationship with religious affiliations. The Religion in Education Foundation (RIE) was Frankl's initial sponsor and made possible Frankl's introduction to academic audiences in the United States. Frankl, however, wanted his theory of Logotherapy to find a legitimate place among psychological

---

[21] Erich Fromm, "The Limitations and Dangers of Psychology," in *Religion and Culture: Essays in Honor of Paul Tillich*, ed. Walter Leibrecht (New York: Harper & Brothers, 1959) 36.

[22] Frankl, Harvard lectures, reel 5, side 1, 22 September 1957.

theory. While he spoke passionately about the limitations of psychology, advocated dialogue, and made an appeal for a more ethically grounded and relevant psychology generally, he saw psychology as the more powerful and legitimate avenue for his theory. His ambiguous relationship with religious affiliations did not go unnoticed. Years later, in a series of letters between the wife of RIE's founding president Randolph Sasnett and Robert Leslie, founder of the Viktor E. Frankl Collection at Graduate Theological Union in Berkeley, California, Frankl's unease with his association to the Religion in Education Foundation is illuminated. On 27 February 1989, Mrs. Martena Sasnett wrote,

> I believe that the very first edition [reference to the publication of *Man's Search for Meaning*] had recognition of The Religion in Education Foundation. Viktor then was glad for any organization related to higher education which could give him an introduction to American audiences through bookings in the College of Medicine in our great universities. Viktor met Gordon Allport when Allport hosted him at Harvard on the first RIE tour in '57.... Now, after Randolph's initial contact with Beacon Press for the manuscript of Viktor's and Allport's scholarly approval, and Beacon's acceptance, then Viktor felt he did not need us anymore. It was apparent that he did not want anything to do with "religion"—in whatever guise—so reference to RIE was sponged from further publications, and Gordon Allport was the one mentioned for his introduction to the U.S. academic scene.[23]

Frankl's lectures at Harvard are important, however, for the following reasons: Frankl is spontaneous in his delivery of many of these lectures, and this provides a rare and valuable glimpse into the interdisciplinary style of Frankl's thought and work; the themes he raises during these lectures resonate with the important dialogue going on between theology and psychology during this time; the lectures address the problems and limitations of psychology; and finally, given the interdisciplinary space Harvard provided, these initial lectures seem to expose Frankl's political and cultural views more poignantly than subsequent writings and lectures he gave in North America in the decades that followed.

---

[23] Mrs. Martene Sasnett to Robert C. Leslie, 27 February 1989, Viktor E. Frankl Collection, GTU 89-5-012, GTU archives, Berkeley CA.

The question-and-answer periods that followed each of the Harvard lectures also provide valuable insight as to how Frankl's theory was received and what themes and questions characterized the dialogue between psychology and theology during this time. They also reveal a general question shared by those gathered as to whether psychology and theology should be engaged in dialogue or whether each had clear and separate mandates. Many in the audience, for example, felt that Frankl was retranslating theological statements within his theory of Logotherapy. From the very first lecture on 20 September 1957, the Harvard audience of both theologians and psychologists felt that Frankl's concept of the spiritual dimension, his notion of transcendence in relation to psychological development, and his statement that each individual life was unconditionally and ultimately meaningful were all clearly theological. The psychologists felt this was problematic, representing an imposition of values, and theological ones at that. As we will see, Frankl answered these concerns from a perspective of ethical responsibility.

Mental Health and Therapy

Let us explore several specific illustrations from these lectures. First, Frankl contended that the construction of psychological categories of illness and disease was contingent upon cultural or social context. As mentioned, Frankl asked his audience the following general question: What gives rise to the belief (not the empirical fact) that neurosis is on the rise? For Frankl, such a belief is a psychotherapeutic leap, because the categories and symptoms of neurosis are contingent upon social, cultural, and historical context. Frankl continued to suggest that the content of delusions, or the delusional ideas of patients, for example, change and were shaped by the climate of the historical period one is speaking about and observing. "The spirit of the age," Frankl stated, "makes itself apparent right into the depth of psychotic mental life."[24] On the one hand, Frankl was suggesting that psychology suffered from its own delusion, a belief in its own empirical infallibility. Psychology was very much in the business of constructing categories of mental illness. Psychology was anything but ahistorical or apolitical. The "spirit of the age" influenced psychology's own belief system and construction of symptoms. Ironically, psychology's powerful hold on

[24] Frankl, Harvard lectures, reel 1, side 1, 21 September 1957.

our collective imagination influenced the belief and perception that these symptoms or illnesses were real and on the rise. The first step, then, was to be aware of the reciprocal influences that produced and perpetuated notions of mental health.

If psychological theory, Frankl stated, absorbed the cultural, political, economic, religious, ethical, and historical contexts in which it was embedded, psychology also had embraced a theoretical style that categorized, if not reduced, human experience to a predictive by-product of these same "environmental" influences. This assumes that the environment is stable and itself not open to reflective analysis. It was this reductive philosophy, Frankl claimed, so widely adopted and popular within many psychotherapeutic models that lead to a contempt for anything moral, spiritual, or religious. Psychology could not, according to Frankl, close its eyes to the "spirit of the age," but neither could it ignore the religious and moral expressions of its clients. These expressions were more difficult to categorize. In fact, they pointed to a very disruptive variable: Much about being human could not be known. While psychology internalized and duplicated social contexts, it simultaneously influenced them. That influence, however, was seen as limited, problematic, and negative. The challenge to psychology was to expand its theoretical boundaries (expand its purpose and mission) while retaining its powerful position as social commentator.

Frankl suggested that the individual stories that emerged through dialogue (not objective interpretation) in therapy were a complex hybrid of subjective experience, subjective moral and ethical expressions, subjective constructions of meanings, values, and beliefs that both mirrored and rebelled against the internalizations of collective social, political, economic, ethical, and religious expressions. This spawned much debate in the Harvard audience about the "confessional" aura of therapy. Many in the audience wondered whether a minister, priest, or rabbi would be able to distinguish a religious enquiry or problem from a psychological one, and, further, know when to refer an individual to a psychologist. The amount of time members of the audience and Frankl spent on this particular subject raises the problematic issue of classifying questions of existence. Frankl's response was that Logotherapy had to act as "medical ministry." Being responsible therapeutically meant being open to the religious and spiritual expressions of clients. Again, the audience of both theologians and psychologists grappled with this. Was a religious or spiritual expression identifiably different from any other expression in therapy? Were deeply felt, sometimes painful questions by a client about the meaning and value of one's life or life generally very different, or was it the answers given to these existence questions that were markedly different? Frankl stated that questioning the meaning and value of life was not a sign of pathology or abnormality but the fullest expression of being human. Inquiries of this nature made by the client in therapy should be addressed by the therapist and considered a legitimate psychological exploration. The dialogue that takes place in therapy, from an existential perspective, revolves around questions of existence and the exploration of the meaning, value, expressions, and possibilities of being human. At its best, therapy offers a space to explore possibilities that become imbued with further meaning and value through dialogue and are potentially brought into concrete reality by the client. Logotherapy aimed at giving secular therapists and doctors a perspective that would enable them to provide a therapeutic setting that did not shut the door to religious or spiritual expressions should the client wish to venture there.

Second, Frankl suggested that patients know too much. As early as the late 1950s, Frankl preceded present-day reflections on psychology by suggesting that a cultural proliferation of psychological terminology in the West was shaping our everyday language, how we saw each other, and the degree to which we internalized notions of human potential. The process of internalizing psychological concepts preceded clients into therapy and influenced not only what the client said but also the outcome of a therapist's interpretation of what was being expressed. Far from being a neutral and objective enterprise, Frankl pointed out two concurrent problems within therapy. First, by the client knowing "too much," the client could inadvertently fit his or her "story" to suit the model or theory used by the analyst. Second, the interpretation of the client's "story" (if an interpretation was given) would fit both the specific approach and underlying concept of human nature at the foundation of the theory adopted by the therapist.

So what was Frankl suggesting? What was problematic about psychology? First, psychology had to confront its elevated status within Western culture. Psychology was not even aware of the degree to which its conceptualizations about human nature were being adopted, often uncritically, by the population at large. If, as Frankl believed, every psychological theory had a specific philosophy of human nature at its foundation, and every psychological theory had a conception of what it is to be human, psychological theories also perpetuated these images. In terms of research, if every psychological theory made claims about what constitutes human growth and development, then these foundational concepts more often than not preceded theory by motivating and framing our initial questions, which, in turn, influenced the outcome of psychological studies and subsequent analysis. In keeping with the growing critique that psychology could well fall toward scientific and emotional determinism, Frankl attempted to introduce a multidisciplinary dialogue to psychology.

Any kind of dialogue or interaction, whether between two people or two disciplines, is invariably a complicated dance, one that involves intent to collaborate, to explore mutual positions, to discover new perspectives, and even to be receptive to substantial change. At the same time, intended collaboration may not be equal, it may produce more questions and more problems, and it invariably runs the risk of one person or one discipline wittingly or unwittingly overcoming the other rather than engaging in a true dialogue. Dialogue may inevitably create more ambiguity and less certainty. This is certainly the case with Frankl. Frankl's psychological dialogue with other disciplines runs in both directions. It is refreshingly provocative as a psychological theory with its openness to dialogue and collaboration, its suggested rethinking of psychology's universal claims and assumptions, and its integration of other perspectives in an analysis of human existence (religion being the most obvious one). But it also runs the very risk psychology was accused of; that is, of analyzing culture, in this case through a Logotherapeutic lens. Despite this, Frankl denounced the increasing overemphasis on empirical and objective science within psychology and called for a more humble interaction between psychology and all cultural discourses.

Psychology as Social and Political Commentator

Despite Frankl's criticism that psychology was increasingly lapsing into generalities, much of his Harvard lectures contain fairly sweeping political generalizations. Clearly, Frankl felt that a psychological perspective that began with the client in therapy and extrapolated to general observations about the wider population yielded a fruitful contribution to political discussion. Frankl announced that not only psychology but politics needed to be humanized. A "spiritual earthquake" contributing to the "poisonous fumes of nihilism"[25] was a potentially global danger, according to Frankl. The Europeans had experienced this historically, and Frankl knew its manifestations: an ephemeral and fatalist attitude toward life, collectivist thinking, and fanaticism, nihilism, and a fear of responsibility. Nihilism was a pervasive attitude, according to Frankl, that an individual's existence was meaningless and valueless. For Frankl, contemporary (Western) humankind was expressing this attitude toward others and toward itself. This experience and expression created what Frankl termed an existential vacuum born of apathy and was concurrent with the increasing social and cultural expectations of the modern world. The pace to keep up, morally and mentally, with social, political, economic, and technological changes, for example, was creating distinctive psychological problems. "Technology," he argued, "is outstripping humanity."[26] Frankl used several analogies to describe these phenomena. First, biological acceleration (the earlier onset of puberty) was equated with several cultural accelerations, causing what he called a puberty crisis within humanity generally. Second, where we once understood "self" as a creature in the image of God, we now saw ourselves in the machine age as both the creator and image of our own creation. Technical conceptualizations of the self, when internalized, led us to believe that we were "nothing but" the product of generalized and quantitative categories. This cultural trend, Frankl believed, paralleled the trend within psychology generally, whereby the client was reduced "to the mere neurophysical realm."[27] This tendency toward a "nothing but" attitude distorted the image of human beings and led to what Frankl felt was a pervasive global expression and attitude of nihilism. In recent history, Frankl told his Harvard audience, "the conception of [man] as nothing but a product of heredity and environment—blood and soil—pushed us all into historical disaster."[28] Our theoretical inventions and conceptualizations were, for Frankl, as dangerous politically and culturally as the concrete weapons we invented to

[25] Frankl, Harvard lectures, reel 1, side 1, 21 September 1957.

[26] Ibid.

[27] Ibid.

[28] Ibid.

destroy each other. Frankl's tone was increasingly one of politician and preacher when he suggested that the gas chambers were not only invented and prepared by the military in Berlin, they were "invented at the desks and lecture halls of nihilistic philosophers and scientists unwittingly making philosophical statements concerning the essence and nature of [man] and thus conveying nihilistic philosophies and philosophical assumptions."[29]

Citing recent history, Frankl stated that the concentration camp, in his opinion, was a microcosmic mirroring of the world. "The concentration camp tore open the human soul and revealed the dichotomous quality of human existence. We were a mixture of good and evil, decent and indecent and this mixture belied the philosophies of pure race."[30] What psychotherapeutic teachings, Frankl asked, could be drawn from the camps? His answer, by way of warning to his Harvard audience in 1957, was our very real, very human capacity to create new concentration camps. Frankl implicated the discipline of psychology and what he called the dehumanizing tendency to reduce human experience to purely quantifiable categories. This tendency to belittle the possibility of transcending a given situation, to deny new potentialities and new meanings, to dismiss faith, and, in effect, to strip human existence of positive value was one avenue toward creating new and repressive concentration camps. The tendency toward cynicism and pessimism that Frankl felt was pervasive in the mid-twentieth century devalued dialogue, relation, and cooperation.[31]

Psychology not only had to be aware of its own constructions—its unwitting statements about the essence and nature of humankind—but, given its prominence within Western culture, it also had to shoulder a social responsibility.

Psychology's Responsibility and the Responsibility of the Therapist

Frankl's psychological prescription for the disease of our time, what he called the dangerous attitude of nihilism, involved all psychologists. Psychologists had an ethical duty to warn against nihilism, and they could

[29] Frankl, Harvard lectures, reel 1, side 1, 21 September 1957.
[30] Frankl, Harvard lectures, reel 2, side 2, 21 September 1957.
[31] Ibid.

only do this by having "an ear to society and culture."[32] This was certainly a different description of and mandate for what a psychologist did. Frankl's call to responsibility had several layers. First, it went against the professional projection that a therapist or psychological researcher was both objective and neutral. Second, it raised what was seen as the problem of psychology's insularity and apolitical, ahistorical stance. Third, it raised the question as to what extent a therapist is a social and moral compass and has a responsibility to guide the client and whether this is inevitable and should be acknowledged. Fourth, it required that psychology become aware of its underlying image of humankind and the impact this image has not only on the individual facing the psychologist, but of the impact these images have within the larger culture and how they are interpreted and used by the larger culture.

If a psychologist had this kind of social and political responsibility, what, then, was psychology's mandate, and, specifically, what was Frankl suggesting as Logotherapy's mandate? Psychology, according to Frankl, must stimulate an individual's search for meaning. This search or striving for meaning in one's life, what Frankl termed the will to meaning, was the primary motivating factor in a person's existence. A Logotherapist, and by extension any psychologist, should stimulate the will to meaning, stimulate the possibility for meaning throughout life, and stimulate an individual's responsibility. A therapist should guide an individual toward a positive goal. A therapist should therefore embody a specific and fundamental posture: that there is something to aim for, the aim or goal should be positive, and this goal of striving forward and toward something or someone is necessary for positive growth and well-being. Clearly, this is a value the therapist embodies and a value the therapist conveys as therapeutically positive to the client. Frankl's Harvard audience immediately voiced concern that these sentiments were a clear imposition of values and that ultimately the therapist would be leading or directing the client in a certain direction. Frankl, however, felt there was a distinct difference between a general valuing of the meaningfulness of life and/or a belief in positive human potential that the therapist should personally embody (and in Frankl's vision, has a responsibility to convey to another human being, especially at a point of crisis) and the imposition of specific

[32] Ibid., reel 1, side 1, 21 September 1957.

guidelines or values the client must follow in his or her particular life. The therapist, specifically the Logotherapist, begins the process of therapy "with the assumption that life is meaningful and that there is meaning to one's existence."[33] Although one can argue that this is a general value about life, Frankl distinguished this from what the client ultimately does by himself or herself. The therapist, Frankl stated, observes the steps, "but the walk itself is performed by the patient."[34]

Psychology, Frankl pronounced, had to remind itself that human beings were not driven beings but deciding beings, free and certainly capable of shouldering responsibility. Frankl saw the role of the Logotherapist as one who assisted the awakening of responsibility within the client. The hope for the client was that he or she would be able to move independently forward, conscious of his or her unique responsibility, conscious of freedom and attitudes, better able to choose and decide, open to discovering potential possibilities or meanings, and, finally, able to implement these things concretely in his or her life.

Logotherapy, Frankl stated, was an education toward responsibility.[35] We were not, Frankl suggested, driven by ego or super ego, not mere products of heredity or environment, but free responsible beings. Logotherapy was seen as a supplement to help or inform disciplines like psychology to enlarge the images of humankind and the presuppositions about humankind that anchor most theory. The idea of transmitting an ethic of responsibility also extended for Frankl to education, theology, and social work. Each of these areas, Frankl believed, faced the existential vacuum of modern man: the frustration, aimlessness, boredom, and meaninglessness that derived from the modern world. An education in responsibility entailed responsibility for our decisions, for our answers, our moral conscience, for society, humanity, and, for some, a responsibility to God.

Being human and acting responsibly meant exercising the existential act, the ability to transcend somatic and psychic circumstances. We were more than mere products of the environment, more than psychodynamics. What made us truly human was the ability to encounter ourselves, to objec-tify ourselves, to oppose ourselves, to be free and responsible agents.

---

[33] Frankl, master lecture manuscript, 21–27 September 1957.

[34] Frankl, Harvard lectures, reel 5, side 2, 22 September 1957.

[35] Ibid., reel 6, side 1, 27 September 1957.

The existential act, the transcendence of the somatic and psychic dimensions, elevated us to the spiritual dimension, the human dimension. Science, on the other hand, was limited to one dimension and, therefore, produced a limited view of human nature. If psychology were to transcend the level of psychodynamics and follow individuals into the human dimension, it would have to confront the spiritual and moral conflicts that develop. For Frankl, psychology had stepped away from these spiritual and moral conflicts.

The Boundary with the Spiritual Dimension: Broadening Psychology's Mandate

Does our existence have meaning? Assuming we are more than psychosomatic or psychosocial dynamics, we exist, but what meaning does our existence potentially have? Frankl's answer was two-fold. First, there is an unconditional meaning to life. Second, we discover meaning through creative, experiential, and attitudinal values. That there is an unconditional meaning to life alludes to an ultimate meaning. Frankl never denied this but was ambiguous as to whether he was implying that our existence points to an ultimate meaning. However, he did suggest that a Logotherapist must convey to the client the sentiment that life generally, and that each individual life specifically, possessed this unconditional meaning and value. Is this somewhat problematic or possibly revolutionary for psychology? It may be the borderland with the religious or spiritual any psychologist faces when another human being sitting before him or her in dialogue raises questions about existence.

Becoming increasingly aware of the attitudes we hold and the contexts that surround them offers the possibility of discovering change, choice, and meaning. Awareness offers the possibility of yet another lens through which to experience and contextualize our attitudes. Awareness offers a degree of distancing so one can utilize one's freedom to decide if a particular attitude offers possibility for growth, healing, and meaning or whether it hinders these same things. An increase in awareness came through dialogue with the therapist and then could extend to the myriad dialogues a client had with the world around him or her. For Frankl, the dialogues we have assume an objective counterpart, and he always left the door open to interpret one's counterpart as God. God was, for Frankl, the partner in our most intimate dialogue: the experience we had of the speaker behind the voice of our conscience who was the ultimate partner in our innermost and deepest dialogues.

Questions about ultimate meaning or the unconditional meaning of human life were questions of existence that brought psychology to the boundary of the spiritual dimension. The meaning of one's existence resided within encounter, within relationship and dialogue with "other." Frankl suggested that healing resides at the level of the spiritual. As finite beings, we are unable to grasp intellectually an infinite and ultimate meaning. At that moment of inability, our thinking process has to yield to belief. Ultimate meaning entailed belief, not intellectualizing. You cannot see the soul through a microscope, Frankl stated, but what motivates you to search is a spiritual interest. There is, in other words, a presupposition in every so-called scientific search that Frankl believed began with a very human and spiritual quest, an innate search for meaning.

This caused one member of the Harvard audience to ask Frankl if he believed there was an overlap between the role of psychologist and the theologian. This, in turn, provoked an audience member to ask about the following: If psychotherapy engaged in this innate striving and search for meaning, and if psychotherapy were to take up the existential questions presented in therapy, then what were the boundaries between psychology and religion? Frankl's response was that psychology, and specifically his theory of Logotherapy, was not explicitly but implicitly dealing with religious questions. Frankl's attempt to distinguish the role of the psychologist from that of the religionist (his term) was always somewhat weak. Religion, Frankl stated, aimed at salvation, while psychotherapy's aim was focused on the health of psychic systems. This, however, contradicted the fact that Frankl placed psychological health and healing squarely within the spiritual dimension, a dimension he added to broaden the concepts of mental health beyond psychic systems. While the fundamental roles of psychologist and theologian were different, Frankl conceded that religion often had an unintended therapeutic side effect and could provide a level of security and anchorage that psychology simply could not. Psychotherapy also had an unintended side effect in that the client might regain a capacity for faith. Frankl made a distinction between what he believed was a human capacity for faith from what was observable or what was known. The observable were givens (be they biological or environmental, for example) and the realm in which a doctor works and through which he or she could not transcend. Yet Frankl also suggested that a doctor could not be a detached observer. A doctor engaged in the immediacy of interpretation, and interpretation was always open to change and ambiguity. Interpreting the "facts" required a doctor to engage in a dialogue between what he or she not only physically observed but also what patients themselves revealed. Medical doctors and psychologists were both bound to the realm of what was seemingly observable and knowable and yet continuously confronted by patients, fellow human beings, who defied equations of cause and effect. A therapist, for example, who met a patient with an attitude of possibility and conveyed a value for the unconditional meaning of life was also conceding that what lay beyond the psychosomatic realm was rather ambiguous and open to faith.

Conclusion

Frankl's theory of Logotherapy was intended to be a supplemental anthropology in the hopes of expanding the horizon and possibilities of established models of psychotherapy. A fundamental issue that had to be addressed was, according to Frankl, the distorted underlying "concept of man" portrayed in most psychological theories. By distorted, Frankl meant the tendency of psychological theories to interpret human existence from a one-dimensional plane, be it scientific or psychodynamic, thereby ignoring what he felt was the multidimensional reality of existence. It was key to become aware of these foundational images, how they guided theory and practice, why they developed, and what their limitations were.

Frankl's adoption of a more interdisciplinary approach and vision to psychology's primary subject, the individual, called attention to the inherent assumptions, values, intent, and multiple contexts that influenced theory and practice. To the audience at Harvard Divinity School in 1957, Frankl spoke passionately about the dignity and uniqueness of individual development and the meaning of existence. The meaning of individual existence, he stated, was contingent upon "my" being objectively challenged, challenged by a standard not of "my" own making. It was through challenge, questions presented, dialogue, and engagement that led to our reaching out beyond our individuality and being ethically motivated to respond to others and the world around us. We were to place ourselves next to these challenges, compare and contrast, engage, find common ground, or possibly rebel. The motivation to search for meaning and the striving to transcend ourselves toward something or someone was connected to what existential analyst Alfried Längle would later identify as our being essentially dialogical; that is, our need and search not only for meaning, but also for dialogue, relationship, and engagement with others. As Frankl stated during the Harvard lectures,

> How ridiculous man becomes the moment he tries to make himself into his own standard, not only morally and spiritually, but also bodily.... This is what [Jean-Paul] Sartre, the French existentialist, is saying when he tells people that "man is inventing himself." This means that man creates his own ideal and grows toward it. As long as such an ideal is created by himself, it can not be a really challenging ideal; it has no imperative—it carries no moral obligation at all.[36]

The questions from the Harvard audience and the answers provided by Frankl, although often ambiguous, suggest the continual conflict and a mutual borderland between psychology and religion. Each addressed aspects of human existence that often overlapped and often did not. The consensus as to whether there should be a clear distinction between the two disciplines was never reached. Even the most dubious in the audience conceded that Frankl was challenging the foundations of psychology and pointing out some profoundly new ways of conceptualizing theory and therapy. Frankl's mid-twentieth-century warnings and concern about the discipline of psychology extended to his commentary on psychotherapists as participants, witnesses, and analysts of history and culture. Psychotherapists were witnesses to the depth of their client's experiences and how those experiences were both influenced by and influenced the social world. Therapists and theorists were collaborators with the greater social environment. Therapists and theorists were possibly cultural activists who embodied certain values and potentially transmitted them.

At the end of one lecture, Frankl left his audience with an open and intellectual challenge. He suggested that psychology's "deliberations must extend out," implying that psychology must engage with the world and that there was, in Frankl's words, a "need for a psychotherapy [capable of preventing] any further spread or repetition of anything like a concentration camp."[37] Frankl's challenge suggested that psychology as a

---

[36] Frankl, master lecture manuscript, 21–27 September 1957.

[37] Frankl, Harvard lectures, reel 3, side 2, 21 September 1957.

discipline was anything but ahistorical or apolitical. Psychology had a foundation in ethics, it had to be more "socially aware," play a greater societal role, be responsive, and contribute.

Dialogue and cooperation between psychologists and theologians in tackling both individual and social ills continued during this period when theologians began to examine the role and influence of psychology in seminary schools and parishes as the Harvard Project on Religion and Mental Health under the direction of theologian Hans Hofmann began in 1956.

4

Hans Hofmann and the Harvard Project on Religion and Mental Health, 1956 to 1961

> M]ental health can conceivably become a common ground and basic criterion for religious, social and cultural vitality. But first of all the concept of mental health needs resolute liberation from any identification with the egoistic mirage of an unconcerned happiness, with a peace of mind that is not mindful that we are always integral parts and responsible members of our society and cultural situation. We cannot be happy or healthy if we do not gain our self-respect and the development of our personal potentials from an active participation in the societal and cultural struggle to rediscover always anew the meaning and purpose of individual and corporate human existence.[1]

Introduction

This chapter's opening quotation by theologian Hans Hofmann conveys a familiar sentiment shared among many theologians and psychologists during the mid-twentieth century. What we think of as well-being is not simply an internal emotive, perceptual, or experiential equilibrium. Individual well-being is, rather, inextricably linked to the well- being of community, if not the continuation and development of human existence itself. Well-being reaches out beyond the individual psyche. Well-being means dialogue, relation, participation, and responsibility. Well-being has ethical undertones. What is interesting about this quotation is Hofmann's suggestion that mental well-being, as he refers to it, could be the common ground between two powerful yet often competing voices within culture. The common ground, or perhaps the

---

[1] Hans Hofmann, "Religion and Mental Health," *Journal of Religion and Health* 1/4 (July 1962): 335–36.

common good, to which Hofmann referred could be discovered and expressed by both theology and psychology if each placed the meaning and purpose of human existence at the forefront of their attention and inquiries.

In 1956, the year before Viktor Frankl came to the United States and lectured for the first time at Harvard Divinity School, Hans Hofmann, associate professor of theology with interests in philosophy, psychology, and the social sciences, was named director of the Harvard University Project on Religion and Mental Health.[2] In very general terms, the project's mandate was to explore and utilize a dialogue between psychology and theology in order to expand and enhance the role of pastoral care within the Protestant ministry. The project sought, through interdisciplinary dialogue, to design and implement strategies and curriculum to better educate and prepare ministers to deal with the personal issues of their parishioners and to meet the societal demands of the twentieth century. To make the ministry relevant for contemporary society, a collaborative effort to question and debate those issues and problems that intersected both the personal and communal lives of minister and parishioner was required. It was hoped that the integration of a more enhanced psychological and sociological education with the theological training ministers received while in seminary school would better prepare them to deal with this pivotal intersection. As we saw in chapter 2, theologians within the New York Psychology Group[3] began expressing a growing demand by members of their respective congregations to deal with issues that were not strictly religious in nature. As we saw in chapter 3, Frankl expressed a similar sentiment, albeit from the perspective of psychologists, when he suggested that therapists were being asked increasingly to deal with issues raised by clients that were not strictly psychological in nature. In both cases, it would seem that neither religion nor psychology on its own was adequately prepared to address these demands. It would also seem that the demands made and the questions asked by parishioners or clients embodied the multidimensional reality

[2] The project was first initiated in 1956. Dr. Hans Hofmann was officially named director in 1957.

[3] The New York Psychology Group of the National Council on Religion and Higher Education, 1941–1945, hereafter cited as NYPG. From the collection of Prof. Allison Stokes of Ithaca College, New York.

that characterized human existence, and both religion and psychology were slow to recognize this and adapt to it.

This chapter explores some of the issues at the forefront of the Harvard project's mandate. Most of the chapter draws on Hans Hofmann's commentaries that precede the project's publications. Reflecting both his own academic and theological interests as well as the cumulative efforts of the project's contributors, Hofmann's writings offer a valuable glimpse of the late 1950s and early 1960s in the United States, a time when there seemed to be a great momentum in the dialogue between psychology and theology.

Dialogue is the key. Despite the many reservations about whether or not there were mutual boundaries between psychology and theology, there was a concerted effort at dialogue as a means to transcend divisions between the two. Issues and concerns about social justice, the common good, and how to restore and maintain a humane world worried both psychologists and theologians. They saw a connection between these cultural and ethical concerns and the psychological and spiritual well-being of individuals. In the introduction to *Making the Ministry Relevant*, Hofmann wrote, "Are we able to live in our world and organize our living together so that we can survive on human terms? In a highly impersonal, mechanized and demanding civilization, are the inner human resources both adequate and also sufficiently mobilized for the attainment of a creative common life?"[4] Hofmann's questions provide the backdrop for this chapter. We pay particular attention to his contributions[5] to the project's publications as

---

[4] Hans Hofmann, introduction in *Making the Ministry Relevant*, ed. Hans Hofmann (New York: Charles Scribner's Sons, 1960) ix.

[5] The final report for the Harvard Project on Religion and Mental Health was submitted in 1961, and although a copy of the final report could not be located, the chapter relies on the series of publications Hofmann wrote and edited that emerged from the committee's work. I had numerous communications with Harvard (university representatives, divinity school archives representatives, and individuals from the department of archives for the university overall) in an attempt to track down the final report from the project. None of these sources could locate the actual report or specific documentation regarding the project. I was directed to the year-end reports submitted annually by the dean(s) of the faculty of divinity. I found one reference in the dean's report from the 1961–1962 academic year that mentioned Dr. Hofmann's submission of the project's final report (http://hul.harvard.edu/huarc/reshelf/AnnualReports.htm; accessed 5 November 2002. For this chapter, I am relying on three specific publications and one journal article: *The Ministry and Mental Health*

they address and highlight many by now familiar and penetrating questions about individual and cultural health. The following four topics will be addressed in this chapter: the Harvard project itself, the question of a relevant ministry, the dialogue between psychology and theology, and the appeal for a just and humane world. As we will see, the Harvard project raised the same questions as the NYPG and Viktor Frankl about what constitutes health and well-being and did so with the same sense of urgency about the development and direction of humanity that we saw previously.

The Harvard Project on Religion and Mental Health

The Harvard Project poses a similar problem to the two previous historical illustrations. There is very little known or written about it, and this influences how one approaches the material. The project's work and Hofmann's direction is cited in several publications on the subject of the church and mental health that appeared in the early 1960s. A general analysis of the project itself, though, or the placing of it within the context of a dialogue between psychology and religion/theology in the mid-twentieth century is virtually non-existent. The chapter will, as a result, focus on Hofmann's own analysis of the situation and the potential worth of the project. This will, it is hoped, expose the scholarly potential contained in yet another historical dialogue between theology and psychology in the mid-twentieth century.

In 1956, at the instigation of the Academy of Religion and Mental Health, the National Institute of Mental Health (NIMH)[6] gave equal yet

---

(New York: Association Press, 1960) and *Making the Ministry Relevant* (New York: Charles Scribner's Sons, 1960), both edited by Hofmann; *Religion and Mental Health* (New York: Harper & Brothers, 1961), which was written by Hofmann; and an article by the same title published in the *Journal of Religion and Health* (1/4, 1962, 319–36). The two books Hofmann edited include contributions by Paul Tillich, Reinhold Neibuhr, Seward Hiltner, Kenneth Appel, and Talcott Parsons.

[6] The National Institute of Mental Health was established in 1949. In 1955, the Mental Health Study Act authorized the NIMH to study and make recommendations on mental health and mental illness in the United States. The act also authorized the creation of a joint commission on mental illness and health. The Mental Health Study Act further authorized the United States Surgeon General to award grants to non-governmental organizations for partial support of a nationwide study and reevaluation of problems of mental illness (http://www.nih.gov/about/almanac/historical/legislative_chronology; accessed 6 November 2002.

separate grants to Harvard, Yeshiva, and Loyola Universities to conduct a five-year interdisciplinary study on religion and mental health. With Hans Hofmann named director of the Harvard project, many familiar names were selected for the board and/or contributed to the project's publications. They included Paul Tillich, then on faculty at Harvard Divinity School and named to the project's board, along with fellow Harvard professors Gordon Allport and Eric Lindemann from the department of psychology and G. C. Homans from sociology. The project produced several publications with chapter contributions from NYPG alumni Tillich, Seward Hiltner, and Gotthard Booth. Other contributors to the project's publications included Reinhold Niebuhr; Earl A. Loomis, a colleague of Tillich's from Union Theological Seminary; Robert C. Leslie, who would later be instrumental in founding the Viktor Frankl Collection at the Graduate Theological Union archives in Berkeley, California; and psychiatrist Kenneth E. Appel, a prominent member of the Academy of Religion and Mental Health during these same years.

An editorial in *Theology Today* announcing the interdisciplinary project at Harvard reported that the grants from the NIMH were precipitated by "the speedy deterioration of mental health among the American people on the one hand and the need to determine on the other hand which agencies in society are most helpful in providing an atmosphere in which mental health can not only be generated but sustained."[7] The editorial went on to point to "religious agencies…as the most strategic," something we would be unlikely to hear today, "since they have a more continuous and relatively intimate relationship with persons than do medical and legal agencies."[8] That being the case, ministers and pastors would benefit from a more expansive education, one which included psychological education. A more relevant ministry would be "instrumental in making the Christian faith a vital reality in the life and society of our time."[9]

Despite the theological bias, the Harvard project was committed to interdisciplinary study and cooperation. Using the word "bridge" to describe the project's primary aim, the initial press release expressed the

---

[7] E. G. Homrighausen, "The Church in the World" (editorial) *Theology Today* 15/1 (April 1958): 1–6.

[8] Ibid., 1.

[9] Ibid.

hope of reducing the gap between theology and psychology. "Theology must become more relevant and the behavioral and natural sciences more concerned about understanding the real human factor. This calls for continuous interdisciplinary teamwork."[10] Interdisciplinary cooperation was deemed necessary in order to address these large concerns and issues. The fact that the project sought an interdisciplinary forum to address issues of individual and community health and well-being provides yet another fascinating historical example of two powerful cultural voices attempting fruitful dialogue. As we will see in the following chapters, more contemporary voices continue to raise similar issues. Although representing different psychological perspectives, critical psychology and existential analysis tackle many of the same issues and concerns about what factors might contribute to a sustained and humane approach to individual and cultural well-being. Contemporary theory, in some quarters, continues to search for what Hofmann called the "real human factor."

The Harvard project was specifically interested in "(1) investigating the problems and potentialities of the Protestant ministry in relation to mental health, (2) designing a curriculum that would incorporate the results of the investigation, (3) the training of seminary teachers who could instruct in the area of mental health, and (4) preparing textbooks to assist in their teaching."[11] Under the auspices of making the ministry relevant, the study spoke to the new role ministers were required to play in the mid-twentieth century and the new preparation they needed for it.

The cultural power and prevalence of psychology influenced the discussions of ministerial relevance and adequate training but also raised several complications. First, the burgeoning field of psychology in the West had made prolific penetrations into everyday language and thought. By the mid-twentieth century, this influence, it was felt, had contributed to a general shift in cultural focus from external community life to the internal psychic dynamics of individuals, with the primacy placed on individual well-being and development. As representatives of a public institution who upheld the Christian ideals of community life for their parishioners, ministers now had to confront a complex contemporary relationship between seemingly private and individual mental health issues and larger

---

[10] Ibid.

[11] Hofmann, "Religion and Mental Health," 319.

cultural and social issues. Ministers were suddenly expected to be adept at handling this complicated relationship and deal with both the individual and communal lives of their parishioners.

Second, the influence of psychological perspectives on theology illuminated the strictly doctrinal position ministers had relied on in the past when faced with the personal issues of their parishioners. These entrenched positions were seen as contributing to the reluctance of the church to meet these new demands. Hofmann wrote,

> The Christian ministry can no longer limit itself to proclamations about God and the world from which ethically correct behavior can be easily derived. Teaching and preaching at people on an exclusively rational level and about all that is outside of [man] is simply no longer sufficient. People no longer worry as much about what is outside of them as they do about what is inside of them. They want to find out whether they themselves are able to stand their ground against the impact from outside. They want to know how all their diverse and at times contradictory facets can be channeled into a total personality constructively interacting with the environment.[12]

By the late 1950s, a singularly doctrinal approach of theology was increasingly seen as inappropriate for parishioners. At the same time, however, one can also see how psychological conceptualizations began to appear more and more frequently to describe and contextualize current issues. We see this in Hofmann's statement concerning our cultural shift from external to internal concerns and the framing of it from the context of the human psyche. Further, it was assumed that a renewed pastoral role would address the "human factor" and that ministers needed to be more cognizant of the complex expressions of human existence. In order to meet this challenge, it was felt that seminary schools needed to expand their curriculum with courses offered in the human sciences. Those working on the Harvard project specifically sought input from Harvard faculty and the courses being offered in the psychology and sociology departments as they designed a curriculum for a "relevant ministry."

Third, the expansion of the human sciences taught in seminary schools was expected to enrich and inform the job ministers were now expected to do. Interestingly, it was also felt that a rigorous and more

---

[12] Hofmann, *Relevant*, ix.

standardized curriculum in the human sciences would also help curtail the other side of the psychology coin, the misuse and piecemeal application of psychological insights to theological matters. Yet psychological paradigms were also influencing the criteria for recruiting students to seminary schools. Mastery in theological doctrine was no longer seen as sufficient for the prospective seminary student and future minister. Seminaries now had to address what criteria would be used to recruit the "right personality" for ministry in addition to providing the relevant training in the human sciences required for an expanded pastoral role. Recruiting the "right personality" for prospective ministry has some interesting parallels with the therapeutic criteria over what kind of person becomes or should become a therapist. Training in a specific therapeutic model often requires the trainee to undergo a rigorous period of analysis. It would be fascinating to know, in this particular instance, what psychotherapeutic model seminary students were expected to fulfill for their personal analysis.

Fourth, beyond the specific working outline, those involved with the Harvard project raised and discussed the interrelationship of individual and community well-being from a position that neither theology nor psychology alone had or could adequately address. Making the ministry relevant required an interdisciplinary approach but one that also looked critically at the shortcomings of both psychology and theology.

Making the Ministry Relevant

Unsettled by the contention that the twentieth century individual was increasingly focused inward, the Harvard project was, much like the New York Psychology Group and Viktor Frankl himself, a strong advocate for the "humane" being, a person responsibly and ethically linked to the world. Thus, the ministry had an important role to play vis-à-vis the individual, but it also had to tend to that world. The call for a more relevant ministry was also a plea to recapture the "real human factor" in order to secure a just and humane world. As a result, mental health and well-being were once again inextricably linked to the ethical health of the world. When the Harvard project began its five-year study, members acknowledged that the world had changed and was continuing to change rapidly. Rapid technological, economic, and social change shaped the questions, debates, and commentary on contemporary society and raised the issue of the continued relevance of the ministry. Needless to say, the debates revealed divisions of opinion. Should the rights and value of the individual be emphasized, and did this necessarily push our attention away from community? Or should we heed the increasing emphasis, elevation, and dependence on economic and political forces that seemed to neglect the dignity and value of each individual life? Hofmann felt the "real human factor" was lost either way, between the dramatic economic, technological, and social change and psychology's influence in directing our focus and attention inward. Recapturing the human factor meant acknowledging the dignity and uniqueness of each individual as he or she was related to and engaged with the world. The drastic social changes Hofmann addressed in each of his introductions to the project's publications were blamed for stripping individuals of the very human qualities that, it was assumed, engendered peaceful and just behavior, responsibility, and community. Once more, we see the search for a way of expressing the interrelational character of human life and the contention that the nexus point between our internal and external worlds was where mental health, well-being, and, by extension, the common good came together. Neither mainstream psychology nor traditional theology, according to Hofmann, had yet to fully recognize and acknowledge this vital key to human development.

The writings of the Harvard project possess a particular tone and many recurring themes. The historical time was described and perceived in terms of chaos, much like the expressions used by members of the NYPG, resulting in unprecedented numbers of people suffering from anxiety. A growing dependence on economic matters and technology was perceived and feared to have overtaken independence, freedom, and critical thought, for example. There was a sense that core values had been lost, a prevailing sense that many "reliable" foundations within society had collapsed, and that there was a breakdown in human interrelatedness. All of these factors led to a feeling that a radical renewal was necessary within Western society and culture. Once again, it is interesting that the words used to describe the time were also couched psychologically in terms of loss, breakdown, and anxiety.

Hofmann cited the increasing importance of economic matters as one example where the human being was manipulated into what he termed a "labor potential." Education too, he felt, was being driven strictly by scientific and technological advances and bypassing the "unique potentials" within "individual promise." The "absolute superiority of scientific and technological advancement," Hofmann wrote, had severely curtailed "the free development of the human personality."[13] The "economic side of modern life," he continued, "has been permitted to become so tyrannical just because [man] has unconsciously lost his ability to assert [himself] as a human being."[14] The consequences could be seen, as Frankl remarked when he spoke at Harvard in 1957 and as Hofmann reiterated, in the physical and psychological problems that had become increasingly prevalent in Western culture. Placing the increase in human distress squarely on the social, political, economic, and technological changes of the time, Hofmann also stated that we were increasingly dependent on psychology, itself a powerful cultural guide, to investigate, understand, and pronounce on these same changes. He stated, "The social sciences and human engineering have produced very impressive machinery of skilled investigation and effective statistical comparison by which they demonstrate the total ramification and implication of this acute human predicament."[15] Yet Hofmann also voiced a familiar concern as to whether psychology could be as helpful as we expected it to be. Was psychology, in fact, capable of objectively analyzing culture and the social systems that produced it in the first place and continued to influence it?

Hofmann added a critique of the contemporary church. It too had, in Hofmann's opinion, "accepted uncritically the economic development in this country" and its effect on the lives of parishioners.[16] Further, "This is more than partly to be explained by the financial dependence of the church upon those who contribute the most and therefore also feel that they should have the most to say about the role of the church. The church, unfortunately, is no different from other institutions in its desire to justify itself through external aggrandizement."[17]

Just as problematic, in Hofmann's eyes, was the fact that the church had uncritically adopted psychological language, which made its way into weekly sermons by ministers who were themselves poorly trained in the social sciences. Those same ministers were expected to pay psychological attention to the personal lives and predicaments of their parishioners.

---

[13] Hofmann, "Outlook" in *Relevant*, 4–5.

[14] Ibid., 8.

[15] Ibid., 6.

[16] Ibid., 8.

[17] Ibid., 9.

Indeed, congregations increasingly demanded such attention, and, in response, according to Hofmann, too many ministers had adopted a limited and uncritical psychological approach:

> It is disastrous that the Christian church should so enviously borrowed—and without any critical judgment—the psychiatric and psychological insights and methods which, in themselves, are merely the result of our inability to tackle problems in the broader context in which they have arisen. Because of their immoderate dependence on psychiatry and psychology, the churches have been driven to consider the individual instead of the community as a whole, the latter being, in fact, their proper function.[18]

The focus on the personal lives of parishioners shifted focus away from communal life and disrupted the church's "proper function," according to Hofmann. In his eyes, the proper function of the contemporary Protestant church was to both concern itself with the internal life of individual parishioners and simultaneously represent and advocate a positive communal life. On the one hand, a relevant ministry had to meet the demands of a contemporary society that was increasingly concerned with the internal health and well-being of individuals. This was in part due to the influence and power of psychology and in part due to the perception of an increasing "spiritual" malaise amongst people that was generally brought on, it was felt, by dramatic economic and technological advances.

To do so, the church required a relevant ministry, one that was increasingly aware of the social factors that were causing a loss of personal meaning and purpose for many individuals. At the same time, such a ministry had to uphold notions of social justice, for example, so that the congregation did not lose sight of their communal life. Both sides had to be balanced by a relevant ministry in order for the "real human factor" not to be diminished.

Making the ministry relevant meant finding a way to collaborate with other disciplines in the human sciences in order to renew the church's role in contemporary society. "The minister," Hofmann wrote, "finds it difficult to be an effective partner in the maintenance and recovery of individual as well as communal mental health as long as he is unclear and insecure about

---

[18] Ibid.

his professional identity and competence."[19] Hofmann felt that seminaries inadequately trained ministers to deal with the "real problems of living." Theological insights on their own were seen as limited when dealing with the daily problems faced by parishioners. "Unfortunately," Hofmann wrote, "the effect of seminary studies often has been to make [the minister] believe that it was essential that [he] consent to the doctrinal and sectarian heritage of [his] particular denomination regardless of [his] personal intellectual and emotional development."[20] Once again, this is a very interesting comment in light of both the self-appraisal and professional scrutiny many therapists undergo. Unlike many psychotherapies that continue to believe in the objectivity of their professional posture, many others feel the therapist is being demanded by the client to be both a human being and a professional. Existential psychotherapies like Alfried Längle's acknowledge the changes a therapist undergoes as an individual, as a human being, with every encounter and dialogue he or she has with a client. Indeed, the process of therapy, much like an encounter with a parishioner, is a unique encounter between two human beings at a particular moment. Hofmann's assessment of a good pastoral approach sounds almost like an approach to good therapy: "Knowledge," he wrote, "has to be personally appropriated and used imaginatively in concrete pastoral situations."[21]

The Harvard project, therefore, proposed that ministers have an expanded education in the social sciences in order to understand their place in forming contemporary society and how individuals saw themselves. Hofmann wrote,

> [T]he prospective minister would acquaint [himself] as thoroughly as possible with the methods and means by which the contemporary social sciences attempt to analyze, diagnose, and prognosticate the individual, social, economic, and political predicament and potentials in which we live and work. A minister is ill prepared for [his] prospective job if [he] has no knowledge or appreciation of the secular forces and developments that mold the way of living, thinking, and feeling of [his] parishioners.[22]

---

[19] Hofmann, "Religion and Mental Health," 320.
[20] Ibid.
[21] Ibid., 328.
[22] Ibid., 323.

Although the final report for the Harvard project could not be located (the report was submitted during the 1961–1962 academic year), several comments by the dean of the faculty of divinity in his report for the academic year 1960–1961 addressed to the president of Harvard University certainly reflect the influence of the project and Hofmann's contributions. The dean began his year-end report with the following:

> Perhaps no other question harasses us more deeply than the simple but embarrassingly difficult one, "Are we really educating students to be competent ministers?" Revolutions have turned the world upside down and have shattered the old forms of thought, faith, and society so radically that preparation for religious leadership in our time is fraught with a thousand questions, extending in every direction. A new age is being born, a new world is being framed, and the [man] who is to stand in the midst of it must be prepared to grapple with the new questions which are being asked.[23]

To meet this new reality in an age of "new consciousness," as the dean described it, the prospective minister "must reach a new level of religious maturity and professional competence."[24]

Mental Health: The Meeting Ground between Theology and Psychology

What is mental health? What are the criteria for determining what constitutes mental health and what becomes ill-health or psychopathology? What else is attached to mental health? As stated, mental health is not simply an inner psychological equilibrium; it also points to ethical behavior and parallels the health and well-being of cultures and nations. Where do psychology and religion meet on these issues? On one hand, Hofmann believed that it was "inevitable that psychiatrists and ministers should find themselves entangled in discussions about the relationship and possible co-operation between psychotherapy and religion. Both address themselves to the problem of human self-understanding and its expression through behavior."[25] Hofmann, echoing Frankl and members of the

---

[23] Year-end report for the academic year 1960–1961 written to the president of Harvard University from the dean of the faculty of divinity. Located at http://hul.harvard.edu/huarc/reshelf/AnnualReports.htm; accessed 7 November 2002.

[24] Ibid.

[25] Hofmann, *Religion and Mental Health*, 310.

NYPG, also asked the extent to which one could really identify a discernable difference between a religious and nonreligious problem. "The border line between religious and nonreligious problems," Hofmann stated, "is as hard to discern as a dividing line between religious symptoms of an underlying psychopathological problem and the psychopathological expression of a genuinely religious dilemma."[26]

It was inevitable that the "shrinking of time and space on our earth," Hofmann wrote, "has brought to an end the era of self-contained isolationism of any profession. We depend on each other."[27] For Hofmann, religion and psychology did have separate boundaries, and their roles were not to be confused with one another. Nevertheless, religion and psychology also were considered natural allies. Many intersections between the two were made in the writings published on the Harvard project. These included: what it meant to be human; our responsibility to ourselves, to others and to the world; dialogue; the interrelational character of humankind; and the idea that positive psychological growth had many parallels with positive religious faith. Mental health was seen as the result of independence, critical thought, and responsive action and membership within one's community and society as a whole. Again, we see very familiar parallels being made between psychological health and positive faith that were raised in the discussions of the NYPG.

Yet religion could not be reduced to merely psychological phenomena, and psychology could not pose as philosophical or religious reflection. Where the two met and could engage in fruitful dialogue was in their presumed mutual ethical concern for the well-being of humanity. Factors that contributed to an individual's mental health and well-being were many and varied. Just as members of the NYPG and Viktor Frankl had previously discussed, defining mental health from a wider context made interdisciplinary dialogue urgent and timely according to those involved with the Harvard project. Mental health corresponded with a humane world and that, it was assumed, was the mutual concern and common ground for both psychologists and theologians. Again, it begs the question as to whether psychology was designed for or could address ethical issues.

---

[26] Ibid., 332.

[27] Hofmann, "Introduction" in *Relevant*, xvi.

As we saw in chapter 3, Frankl believed psychology was not adequately prepared to delve into this arena.

Mental health, Hofmann believed, could conceivably provide the common ground between religion and psychology. Moreover, the intersection between religion and psychology might just reveal the bridge between the freedom to discover oneself while simultaneously "molding the world in the image of its highest potential."[28] If both minister and psychologist held such a view, how might their dialogue be mutually beneficial? A given minister, for example, might refer a particularly troubled member of the congregation to a psychologist or psychiatrist. Unlike the psychologist—at least at the beginning—the minister would have a vast body of knowledge about the parishioner. He would know, for example, a great deal about the parishioner's family and about its social and economic contexts. Indeed, the minister's dealings with the parishioner would likely extend to knowledge about the parishioner's personality, including opinions and viewpoints that parishioner held. The minister would then be in a privileged position, much like the psychologist. But do psychology and theology in fact have a common goal? Do ministers and psychologists see the mental health and well-being of the individual in the same way? Hofmann stated that the clergy's "prime interest is in the restoration of an active member of [his] congregation" and that "[he] expects the psychiatrist's skill to work toward this end."[29] The minister saw the parishioner as an active member of a social institution and assumed that the psychiatrist, in order to treat a patient, isolated that individual's experiences and activities from the social world in order to focus exclusively on the inner self. "The psychotherapist," on the other hand, "views [his] patient as an individual in need of better self-realization and more satisfactory relation to [his] life setting. [He] focuses on the individual and [his] specific problems. Only in this light, and secondary to the individual's needs, comes the consideration of first [his] familial, then [his] social and professional, and then [his] religious affiliations."[30] The two fields would seem therefore to be quite distinct, as each "attends" to a different aspect of human need. Hofmann appears to have been envisioning

[28] Hofmann, *Religion and Mental Health*, 335.
[29] Ibid., 330.
[30] Ibid.

a way to maintain these distinct roles and also to increase the dialogue, trust, and mutual interests that psychology and theology held. Dialogue would highlight the multiple needs individuals and communities have as expressions of being human.

The Appeal for a Just and Humane World

Sounding very much like Viktor Frankl, Hofmann wrote, "Every human being has the innate and irrepressible urge to make sense of life and to have this sense expressed through the unique character of [his] own personality and in the precise context in which [he] lives and works."[31] The emphasis Hofmann placed on personal meaning and purpose was coupled with the question of how these could be discovered and expressed both at the individual level and in the company of others. Hofmann was critical of a contemporary notion that people know how to live meaningful and ethical lives, that they know when and how to rely on their insights, knowledge, and experience to do the right thing. Each individual supposedly had the internal capacity, fortitude, and desire to do this. A dangerous presumption, Hofmann declared, and, like Frankl, one only needed to look at the increased demand for psychological help for proof. "The psychiatrists' offices," Hofmann wrote, "are full of people who have lost their sense of meaning and purpose for their lives and, therefore, are confused. These people drift listlessly, pushed around by external value suggestions and vague external expectations with which they identify, since they do not know how to discover their inner sense of direction."[32] What is interesting about this comment is Hofmann's awareness of the fact that psychiatrists, as Frankl too had observed, were suddenly confronted with questions about the meaning of life, the meaning and purpose of an individual's life, and how that individual could live meaningfully and ethically within the world. Equally interesting is Hofmann's awareness that the external world played a large part in the mental make-up of the individual patient the psychologist or psychiatrist had seated before them. Trying to bridge the dignity of individual life and the common good seemed to be a recurring question without precise answers. Hofmann

[31] Hofmann, *Relevant*, viii.

[32] Hofmann, *Religion and Mental Health*, 332.

commented on this problem when he stated, "Neither a democracy nor a church can survive if its constituency degenerates either into an amorphous conglomeration of isolated individuals or an equally undifferentiated mass of impersonal nonentities. In contrast to irresponsible individualism or mass anonymity, the people are inter-related, mutually responsive and responsible members of a group with many diverse gifts and functions."[33]

Believing the issue of mental health provided a meeting point between theology and psychology, Hofmann offered several specific areas for exploration. These included the overcoming of narcissistic preoccupation, love, independence, ethical and moral criteria, and religious values that were relevant to mental health. Much like Tillich and Frankl, Hofmann also saw our involvement with and response to the world as an ethical act, indeed, an obligation. We had an obligation to be involved with society and be involved with ethical and moral decisions that affected us all. That kind of engagement, which Frankl saw as pivotal not only to psychological health and development but also to the healthy continuation of the human race, is also Hofmann's as he attempted to bridge the respective mandates of theology and psychology. Involvement with the world or, as Tillich would say, to be ultimately concerned, "can free a person from an undue, narcissistic preoccupation with [his] personal mental health or neurotic tendencies. A realistic religious faith can, therefore, allow a person to see [himself] and [his] difficulties in their actual proportions and dimensions."[34] Contextualizing not only our lives within the greater world, but contextualizing our own problems, leads to a more realistic picture of our place and purpose in the world. Ideas such as these, common to Tillich, Frankl, and Hofmann, also appear in Alfried Längle's theory of existential analysis, as do notions of love. Our ability to love ourselves as well as others was a significant human characteristic, according to both Erich Fromm and Paul Tillich. Hofmann agreed and saw it as a common thread between theology and psychology: "Theology sees in [man's] ability to love the fruition of [his] faith in active and constructive participation in the affairs of [his society]. Psychotherapy recognizes in [man's] ability to love the key toward [his] harmonious self-realization and satisfactory

[33] Ibid., 333–34.
[34] Ibid., 331.

interaction with [his] world."[35] Positive psychological growth manifested itself in emotional maturity and the ability to think independently and critically. Hofmann suggested that religious faith, if positive, would support a similar independent growth. Religious values that corresponded with mental health were those related to the change in attitude we were prepared to make toward ourselves, toward others, and our sociocultural development. Orienting our existence away from mere inner reflection to creative and active involvement and concern with the world around us was, according to Hofmann, the result of positive religious faith and an expression of positive mental health. This same idea of fashioning our existence in an ethical manner toward the world around us is taken up in Alfried Längle's theory of existential analysis, which we will see in chapter 6.

At the heart of so many of these mid-twentieth-century dialogues was a genuine and vocal appeal for social justice and a commitment to human potential. On one level, these dialogues assumed that human beings possessed an ethical foundation and were, in fact, oriented toward the common good. This did not imply that human beings always acted ethically but that they possessed an awareness of and a striving for change, a consciousness that Tillich had described in the NYPG meetings as the human ability to say, "I could have done better." Hofmann wrote, "Human life-awareness begins with the elemental questions of 'why' and 'what for.' The very asking of these questions is the breadth of human dignity. In a society where no one dares to ask them, or where anyone who does is ostracized as an unproductive dreamer, it is clear that we have already succumbed to a total organization under remote control."[36]

Underlying these dialogues between theologians and psychologists was the belief that external social and cultural influences of the twentieth century, notably the Second World War, and then, through the 1950s, the Cold War, with its very serious threat of nuclear war, had eroded mankind's ethical foundations and had eroded the human potential for purposeful striving. Dialogue and relationship, the cornerstones of humane interpersonal encounter, were seen as crucial human characteristics whose potential for expression had been suppressed under the weight of

---

[35] Ibid.

[36] Hofmann, *Relevant*, 12.

social change. Sounding very much like Frankl and others, Hofmann clearly thought that psychology and theology had something to say to each other.

What continues to be fascinating are the complications arising from interdisciplinary dialogue. The influence of psychology, as we have seen in these three historical examples throughout the book, was (and continues to be) so pervasive that internal psychological life became the focus of overcoming the impersonal and dehumanizing social world. At the same time, there was a genuine concern that the focus of turning inward also blinded us to our moral obligation as human beings, that being a responsibility for the common good. These complications, as we shall see in the next chapter, reemerge in critical psychology when postmodern theory also gets tangled between advocating for individual potential and appealing to a collective goal of social justice. Hofmann stated the following:

> It goes without saying that such courage, strength and decisiveness is most needed in a time when the social, economic, and political ideologies have their power backed up by the threat of physical extinction. In this time of totalitarian terror and ruthless economic competition, it is urgently needed that there be a group of people who do not strive to impress their environment through their own qualities of wealth, intellectual brilliance and personal achievements. Their secret is the rediscovery of their purely human ability to live meaningfully and to express their meaningful life in constructive living together.[37]

Conclusion

Hans Hofmann's direction of the Harvard project entailed what was considered a visionary proposal for seminary training in light of contemporary twentieth-century life. Without the final report, we cannot speculate on the extent to which the project's mandate met its goals or implemented real change in curriculum and thinking amongst Protestant seminaries. This chapter's aim was to extricate and highlight the tone and emphasis of the project in order to illuminate this little known but important historical project on the dialogue between psychology and theology. As we have seen in these first chapters, many psychologists and theologians committed

[37] Hans Hofmann, "Immortality or Life," *Theology Today* 15/2 (July 1958): 11.

themselves to very complex issues and questions. The devotion and intensity of their discussions attests to this commitment.

Hofmann outlined a two-fold problem facing both psychology and theology when confronting the topic of human existence. Speaking at the first symposium of the Academy of Religion and Mental Health in 1957, Hofmann stated, "What I call scientism, or the evolutionary illusion, is one expectation that has deluded modern [man] into believing that merely through [his] scientific discoveries and technological advances [he] could eradicate all [his] difficulties and re-create the world and the people in it into a close approximation of [his] ideal of the way things should be."[38] Commenting on religion in the same presentation, Hofmann stated, "A second hope that has disappointed this generation is the belief that, by adhering to the dogmatism, liturgy, and moralism of traditional religion, we will produce [men] who are really human and will thus be able to build a new world full of better people."[39]

Throughout the twentieth century, various interdisciplinary dialogues between theology and psychology implicitly and explicitly stated that neither discipline was well equipped to fully address what it is to be human. In an address to the 1954 meeting of the American Psychiatric Association, Dr. Kenneth Appel (later to become a contributor to the Harvard project) challenged the audience by stating the following:

> If we analyze the brain into chemical constituents and energy transformations, does that mean that thought, feeling, aspiration, loyalty, devotion and love are not real? They are real aspects of experience though they cannot be weighed or measured. How much does loyalty weigh—or reliability? What are the radioactive equivalents of reliability, responsibility, devotion to the well-being of society?[40]

A decade later, following in the footsteps of the Harvard project, Dr. Edward Auer reminded his fellow participants at the 1963 symposium of the Academy of Religion and Mental Health (ARMH) that Appel's challenge to colleagues in the field of psychology and psychiatry had been

---

[38] Hans Hofmann speaking at the 1957 symposium on "The Joint Role of Religion, Behavioral Sciences, and Medicine" in *Religion, Science and Mental Health* (New York: New York University Press, 1959) 54.

[39] Ibid.

[40] Kenneth E. Appel, "The Present Challenge of Psychiatry," *American Journal of Psychiatry* 111 (1954): 1–12.

considered visionary but "actually becomes more of a reality each day."[41] The Harvard Project on Religion and Mental Health is situated among several visionary dialogues that took place beginning with the NYPG in the 1940s. These groups continued, with the ARMH gathering in the early 1960s. Paul Tillich, Hans Hofmann, and Viktor Frankl belonged to the ARMH and through this organization they continued their enduring commitment to dialogue and expanding our discoveries and analyses of human existence. The Harvard project highlighted the potential of dialogue between theology and psychology, where each could learn from and enhance the other's commitment to the welfare of all human beings.

We now turn to several more contemporary voices within the discipline of psychology and discover that many of the mid-century themes of personal and collective well-being explored in this chapter and previous chapters are still very much with us.

---

[41] Dr. Edward Auer speaking at the 1963 symposium on "Moral Values in Psychoanalytic Education and Practice." A summary of the symposium's proceedings in Academy of Religion and Mental Health's *Moral Values in Psychoanalysis: Proceedings of the Sixth Academy Symposium* (New York: Academy of Religion and Mental Health, 1965) 19.

5

Contemporary Issues: The Challenge of Critical Psychology

> The therapeutic gospel celebrates all that promotes self-realization and condemns all that promotes psychological harm. This therapeutic morality, of course, focuses our attention on the private life, blinding us to the larger, public good.[1]

Introduction

In the previous chapter, we saw an illustration of theologians and, by extension, seminary schools coming to terms with the rise in influence of psychological theory. The aim of the Harvard Project on Religion and Mental Health was to integrate psychological perspectives into theological education in order to make religion (specifically Protestant denominations) more relevant to parishioners and equip ministers with therapeutic tools to better serve their communities. At the same time, contributors to the Harvard project voiced concerns about psychology's aim, purpose, and growing influence on our perceptions of self and other. The quote that begins this chapter expresses a present-day but ongoing concern that psychology predominately focuses on the individual and neglects the community or social context in which individual well-being is simultaneously embedded. What does health and well-being really mean if it is stripped of context and relatedness? Expanding upon Eva Moskowitz's statement in this chapter's opening quote, does psychology have an obligation to bridge the lives of individuals with the public good? In treating individuals in therapy, should psychologists be not only aware of but also obligated to acknowledge the patient's role in society? By the same token, to what extent is psychology already coordinating, if not

[1] Eva S. Moskowitz, *In Therapy We Trust: America's Obsession with Self-Fulfillment* (Baltimore MD: John Hopkins University Press, 2001) 7.

manipulating, ideas of psychological health, development, and individual fulfillment with cultural ideals of societal health and productivity?

On one level, psychology does both of these. Theoretical classifications of psychological health and ill-health infiltrate and influence society's general beliefs about many things, including the following: what is normal and acceptable human behavior, what are normal and acceptable displays of feelings or emotions, what constitutes appropriate behavior toward others and toward our family, and what constitutes a positive and healthy relationship with another human being. Psychology does this and also ignores the extent to which it imposes rather grand and generalized ideology, if not morality, about human nature and society while claiming scientific neutrality to justify its aims. The implicit values, belief systems, philosophies, images, and ideologies about human existence within psychology are, however, fascinating. While psychology grew in stature and influence throughout the twentieth century, so, too, did reflective discussions both within and outside of the discipline about the aim and function of psychology. The previous three chapters illustrated several of these interdisciplinary dialogues and discussions. In each case, concern was raised about psychology's increasing and exclusive alignment with scientific paradigms and whether that would ultimately negate its ability to capture the essence of what it was to be human.

This chapter explores two areas. First, we will look at more contemporary voices from within the discipline of psychology that examine its aim, function, and value. Second, we will transpose Paul Tillich's concepts of faith as ultimate concern and the courage to be along with Viktor Frankl's notion of responsibility onto some current debates within the postmodern approaches in critical psychology. It is my contention that much of the current concerns about psychology—both within postmodern theory and without—with regard to the meaning of health and well-being are lingering questions raised by mid-twentieth-century theologians and psychologists that remain essentially unanswered. These questions and deliberations continue to resonate, albeit unconsciously, in the considerations of critical psychology.

Recurring Problems and Debates

What is psychology? What does it do? What are the implicit aims and assumptions that fuel psychological theory, studies, and therapy? Is psychology science? Is psychology too reliant on empirical methodology? Is psychology in the business of ethics? Is psychology, as critics charge, an ahistorical, apolitical enterprise? How can psychology become more socially aware? Is there such a thing as a discernable "self"? Is psychology engaged in producing responsible citizenry? If these questions sound familiar, they are, for many contemporary debates within psychology are reformulations of similar questions and concerns raised throughout the twentieth century. There are, however, several qualifying remarks that must be made. First, while postmodern approaches like critical psychology, for example, have raised important questions and debates for the discipline of psychology, its critique that psychology has removed its object of study from relevant social, historical, political, and ethical contexts is compounded by the fact that it too neglects historical debates, particularly dialogues with theologians or with the existential psychotherapies. Although the desire for interdisciplinary collaboration exists, many within the field of psychology continue to disregard collaborations with scholars in the fields of religious studies, theology, or pastoral counseling. This may be due to psychology's general tendency to ignore or minimize religious and theological contributions.

Second, many of the same ambiguous and complex questions that remained largely unanswered decades ago reemerge within contemporary discussions and reproduce the same ambiguous positions. These include trying to theoretically straddle notions of individuality and the collective (these being perpetually seen as diametrically opposed to one other); analyzing the impact that ideal images of human existence and behavior have on psychological theory; and, finally, seriously reflecting on the extent to which Judeo-Christian ethics are retranslated into psychological theory. Many within the field of psychology of religion, for example, see these subtle ethical retranslations as ultimately problematic. This is so much the case that reflecting on any Judeo-Christian subtext within psychological theory and its potential for creative dialogue and analysis is considered biased scholarship and the "caretaking" of a Judeo-Christian perspective.[2] Yet many so-called secular psychologists, particularly therapists, have written passionately in the last decade about psychology's neglect of issues such as responsibility, community, social justice, and the care for others,

[2] David Wulff, *Psychology of Religion: Classic and Contemporary Views* (New York: John Wiley and Sons, 1991) 11–32.

issues grounded in a Judeo-Christian legacy. What moral and ethical subtext might these psychologists be unconsciously championing?

Why is psychology perpetually apprehensive about responsibility, for example? In his book *Soul Searching: Why Psychotherapy Must Promote Moral Responsibility*, author William J. Doherty provides an astute and somewhat humorous observation on the separation between psychology's promotion of individual rights and its simultaneous dismissal of individual responsibility and participation in community. He writes,

> Although therapists do not tell clients to be politically passive, I see many therapists negatively interpreting their clients' public-service sensibilities and activities. One of Anna's therapists suggested that she was not so much serving other families through her teaching as trying vicariously to heal her own family. A friend told me of his meeting with a therapist just before he departed for Northern Ireland to work with war-oppressed children in the early 1970s. The therapist suggested that my friend was doing this work to deal with the internal war of his own childhood. A colleague curtailed her social activism after her therapist reframed it as a misguided effort to fill a hole inside herself by trying to save the world. I have heard these and other stories continually since I began speaking with other professionals about community commitment and began honoring these commitments among my clients. I met a social activist who builds community and focuses attention on social and environmental issues by means of community involvement projects. He has been told by two personal therapists, as well as by the many therapists in his friendship circle, that his social activism stems from unfinished personal business. When he takes care of his personal business, so the line goes, he will stop acting out his missionary zeal in the world.
>
> All of these socially committed individuals appreciate that their personal issues are involved in their choice of work—as they are for all of us, including therapists. But they understandably resent being patron-ized and pathologized for their energetic work to make a difference in promoting the civil society. When clients tell us they want to change the world, we see them as cosmically co-dependent. A stint of good psychotherapy will send them back to their private world where they can criticize "society" without doing anything about it.[3]

---

[3] William J. Doherty, *Soul Searching: Why Psychotherapy Must Promote Moral Responsibility* (New York: Basic Books, 1995) 98–99.

Not only are individual expressions, experiences, and responses of care toward others minimized, the personal meaning and value derived from these experiences, in addition to possible overlapping religious or spiritual commitments expressed by a client in therapy, continue to be seen through a lens of psychopathology.[4] Again, the fact that many contemporary therapists have published books that address this problem attests to its continuation. In his book *Minding Spirituality*, Randall Sorenson comments that therapists have to take a patient's expressions of spirituality seriously.[5] "Religion or spirituality," Sorensen continues, "has historically received problematic treatment from analysts as have few other expressions of cultural diversity, including socioeconomic status, race, ethnicity, gender, or sexual orientation."[6]

Humanistic and existential psychologist Kirk Schneider sees a danger in what he calls the "epistemological anarchism"[7] of postmodernism. Advocating a "science of humanism"[8] within psychology to counter postmodern positions that "all beliefs are foundationless, all reality is socially constructed, and all views are equivalent in their essential value,"[9] Schneider comments, "I fear for the children growing up in our post-modernistic cacophony; where will they learn emotional and intellectual depth, interpersonal commitment, and enduring values"?[10] These three therapists express what they see within the confines of therapy, and it speaks volumes about what psychology perpetually wishes not to address. Yet conversations of responsibility, values, and community concern and involvement are part and parcel of discussions many therapists have with their clients. A client's ethical posture is very much a part of therapeutic dialogue.

Personality psychologist Robert Emmons feels that "ultimate questions of meaning and existence, purpose and value, do find expression in one

---

[4] Randall Lehmann Sorensen, *Minding Spirituality* (Hillsdale NJ: Analytic Press, 2004) 25.

[5] Ibid., 1.

[6] Ibid.

[7] Kirk J. Schneider, *Rediscovery of Awe* (St. Paul MN: Paragon, 2004) 1.

[8] Ibid., 7.

[9] Ibid., 6.

[10] Ibid., 7.

form or another."[11] These questions are being asked and expressed by clients in therapy, yet psychology continues to ignore, minimize, or even pathologize these same expressions. Addressing his own confrontation with this, Emmons writes,

> When I began my research program on goals, I had no professional interest in religious or spiritual issues. I was content to superimpose existing psychological categories onto what I was trying to understand. Yet because it is such a pervasive dimension of life, spirituality revealed itself repeatedly through the phenomena I was studying—personal goals, well-being, happiness, purpose, meaning, the psychology of possibility and human potential.... As a personality psychologist who professed a desire to understand the person in his or her entirety, I was guilty of ignoring what for many people is precisely what makes their life meaningful, valuable and purposeful. I was ignoring people's attempts to contact a deep and authentic source of striving, goals that came closer to defining who people say they are.[12]

Contemporary approaches to psychology reflect many varying viewpoints on the discipline's problematic response to its main object of study. We now take a closer look at critical psychology, a postmodern vocal and controversial contribution to many of the same questions and debates about psychology's powerful place within our culture.

Critical Psychology

Critical psychology has emerged from critical, social-constructionist, postmodern, and feminist theories, to name but a few. Critical psychology, as an approach, analysis, and critique of the discipline of psychology, is extremely broad and diverse. While critical psychology invites a multidisciplinary approach to this endeavor, it has yet to fully engage with many disciplines that border psychological theory, such as religious studies, theology, or pastoral counseling, for example. Indeed, critical psychology, to date, tends to ignore much of therapy itself in addition to the humanistic and existential psychotherapies. The scant commentary within critical psychology on the existential psychotherapies tends to

---

[11] Robert A. Emmons, *The Psychology of Ultimate Concerns* (New York: Guilford Press, 1999) 6.

[12] Ibid., 7.

confuse them with traditional continental existential philosophy. Because of this, existential psychotherapies are considered part of psychology's continuing problem, the elevation and promotion of individualism, and are, therefore, minimized. In fact, existential psychotherapies stress, and have always stressed, the interrelational reality of human life. Despite these omissions and the lack of any formal or unified theory, critical psychology does, however, raise important questions about the implicit aims and assumptions of psychological theory and practice and why these, in turn, have not been subject to self-reflective analysis.

Current theories in critical psychology have argued that psychological theory has elevated the concept of the individual to a static unit of objective study. This elevation or compartmentalization has, in turn, created and perpetuated a discipline—psychology—that is both ahistorical and apolitical. Critical psychology proposes an acknowledgment of relation and context. This includes the implications of social, political, and economic influences on "individual" experience. It has been suggested that psychology must become socially aware, and this pushes psychological theory to confront its own moral aims and obligations.

The pervasiveness and power of psychological terminology in Western culture is obvious. Psychology shapes how we see ourselves and how we see others. Psychology categorizes our behaviors and emotions and defines what constitutes health, well-being, normal and abnormal behavior. All of these categories and demarcations, presented by psychology as "science," never-theless have deeper ethical, cultural, and political implications. The "culture" of psychology posits more about who we should be, who we want to be, how we should behave, and how a society should conduct itself. Further, critics suggest that the extent to which psychology places its emphasis and focus on individual fulfillment results, as Eva Moskowitz remarks in this chapter's opening quote, in a diminishing of interconnectedness and responsibility.

As we have seen in the previous chapters, it is not a new concept that psychology has increasingly turned a blind eye to ethical issues of responsibility, community, social justice, and care. Debates in the past about psychology and the nature of psychological help continually illustrated the tendency of psychology to ignore religious, spiritual, and ethical issues despite the fact that clients seeking therapy—psychology's main object of study, after all—embody and express these issues in behavior, thought, emotion, and experience. Contemporary debates about psychology continue to raise the perpetual and thorny issue about the extent to which psychology should be engaged in these areas without becoming overt in directing those who seek psychological help (or theorists designing psychological studies) to follow prescribed ethical guidelines. Many critics, however, argue that psychology is already engaged in dictating what the "good life" is, and underneath psychological categories of both health and disease are fairly overt ethical yardsticks for behavior at the individual, family, and societal levels.

Psychology's tendency to promote the primacy of the individual and so-called "individual" experience over and above social, familial, and historical contexts has created an ideal of human development. Edmund Sullivan states, "The ideal person [within psychology] is considered a self-contained individualistic system rather than an interdependent system."[13] The result can be seen in a pervasive ideology within psychological theory, one that assumes (if not creates) an ahistorical, apolitical individual who has the right, capability, and freedom to self-actualize over the course of a lifetime. These individual rights, freedoms, and capabilities are seen outside of any relational context, and this begs the question as to whether these rights and freedoms are uniform and accessible to all. Increasingly divorced from the social world, psychological theories idealize and promote this self-actualizing individual, whose goal is happiness and fulfillment, which are ambiguous terms at best. Positive psychological development revolves around an individual "feeling good," and any aspirations and/or contributions a person makes in the world rests on whether these activities will make ME happy and self-actualized. Frank Ferudi adds that "the feeling of contentment is increasingly seen as the defining feature of individual health.... The emphasis which our emotional script attaches to feeling good about oneself is a distinct feature of contemporary culture. It is underpinned by an outlook that regards the individual self as the central focus of social, moral and cultural preoccupation."[14] And yet the existential analyst Ernesto Spinelli feels that what we deem to be "our problems" are, in fact, not our own "in any exclusively personal sense, in that they are not

[13] Edmund Sullivan, *Critical Psychology and Pedagogy: Interpretation of the Personal World* (Toronto, Canada: OISE Press, 1990) 4.

[14] Frank Furedi, *Therapy Culture: Cultivating Vulnerability in an Uncertain Age* (London: Routledge, 2004) 31.

derived from some internal or intrapsychic set of conditions but, rather, exist at the nexus or meeting point between each person and the world of others which he or she inhabits."[15]

While promoting individual freedom and self-actualization, psychological theory simultaneously constrains human behavior by assuming logi-cal and predictive patterns of behavior and development. Such assumptions are, in turn, legitimized by scientific study and then perpetuated and applied through psychological practice. Indeed, these generalizations creep into our public consciousness and influence everything from health care to education to social policy. Psychological theories and studies are believed to provide accurate accounts of who we are, how we think, and how and why we behave in certain ways. We have come to believe that these theoretical categories and demarcations of human experience are real, fixed, and never-changing. We rarely question the conclusions of psychological studies and have become dependent on the results to dictate the direction of our lives. Voices within critical psychology, however, feel that statistical generalizations limit our potential knowledge of human beings at both the individual and societal levels. Charles Tolman suggests that "a psychology that deals with averages in the hopes of achieving generality through abstraction can never be relevant to the particular individual."[16] Similarly, Lois Holzman comments that the natural scientific model adopted by psychology is "unsuitable and ineffective when it comes to human social phenomena."[17] Of even greater danger is psychology's taking its own entrenched assumptions and priorities as scientific truth and "blindly reproducing them in the ideas of organized science, that is, in theory and method."[18] Critics suggest that

---

[15] Ernesto Spinelli, *The Mirror and the Hammer: Challenges to Therapeutic Orthodoxy* (London: Continuum, 2001) 9.

[16] Charles W. Tolman and Wolfgang Maiers, *Critical Psychology: Contributions to an Historical Science of the Subject* (Cambridge: Cambridge University Press, 1991) 5.

[17] "A Decade of Postmodern Psychology" in *Postmodern Psychologies, Societal Practice, and Political Life*, eds. Lois Holzman and John Morss (New York: Routledge, 2000) 5.

[18] Tolman and Maiers, *Critical Psychology*, 5.

psychological theory "organizes and legitimizes"[19] behavior and actions, that it intervenes in and acts to regulate lives.[20]

Critical psychology thus mounts a serious and important critique of the scientific pretensions of psychology. It also attacks a major tenet of psychology, the primacy of the individual. Sullivan links this to the "methodological individualism" of science itself.[21] The isolated, self-contained individual then lives a psychological life (created for him or her by psychology) "that is largely ahistorical and apolitical."[22] Further, the primacy psychology places on self-determination and self-actualization diminishes, some argue, the value of and need for "collaboration, caring and social justice."[23]

Some critical psychologists, reflecting postmodernism, even question whether there is any individual self left to be analyzed. They allude to an "erosion of the centered self"[24] and to a sense of self as being "constantly re-organized."[25] Both statements imply that personal identity is not static and cannot be clearly defined. As a consequence, interestingly, things that were traditionally associated with personal identity, such as beliefs, values, and meanings, are equally subject to constant reorganization and become ambiguous. And yet there are voices within critical psychology asking for a renewed emphasis on values of responsibility, community, and care.

Psychology's failure to recognize and incorporate the significance and impact of the relational reality between individuals and the world around them is another major criticism critical psychology has mounted against the discipline. For critical psychologists, there is no such thing as an autonomous individual or a unique subject who can be objectively isolated and studied apart from social, familial, historical, and political contexts. Human beings exist in relation and cannot be understood apart from a

---

[19] Ibid., 4.

[20] *Postmodern Psychology*, eds. Holzman and Morss, 5.

[21] Sullivan, *Psychology and Pedagogy*, 4.

[22] Isaac Prilleltensky and Geoffrey Nelson, *Doing Psychology Critically: Making a Difference in Diverse Settings* (New York: Palgrave Macmillan, 2002) 6.

[23] *Critical Psychology: An Introduction*, eds. Dennis Fox and Isaac Prilleltensky (London: Sage Publishing, 1997) 8.

[24] Kenneth J. Gergen, *The Saturated Self* (New York: Basic Books, 2000) xiv.

[25] Tod Sloan, *Damaged Life: The Crisis of the Modern Psyche* (New York: Routledge, 1996) 7.

"dynamic social reference."[26] Behavior, emotions, values, and meanings, for example, have specific reference points as we direct ourselves, and are directed, both inwardly and outwardly. This concern is well voiced by existential psychologist Ernesto Spinelli when he suggests that the discipline needs to adopt self-criticism and social awareness. The "contextualizing presence of the world"[27] needs to be made explicit in both theory and practice. The idea of social awareness implies moral aims and obligations, an area of inquiry rarely addressed in either psychological theory or practice.

Moreover, psychology's emphasis on the self-contained, predictable individual negates human possibility and potential. Rubin feels that the emphasis on the individual within psychology results in the promotion of "excessive self-centeredness and eclipses certain possibilities and features of subjectivity, such as self-transcendence and spirituality, or non-self-centric modes of being."[28] Prilleltensky similarly suggests that "too much self-determination degenerates into individualism and disregard for the well being of others."[29]

In summary, critical psychology argues that the discipline of psychology has ignored cultural, political, and historical context and has instead focused itself theoretically on Western ideals of individualism. The primacy of value placed on individual fulfillment has, in turn, oriented notions of psychological health and well-being around the attainment, if not goal, of self-determination or self-actualization. The view that psychology has perpetuated a theoretical division between what sounds like the inalienable rights of the individual to self-actualize over and above our human obligations and responsibilities to "other" is voiced often within critical psychology. Richardson, Fowers, and Guignon comment on the effect this valuing of individual fulfillment has on approaches to family therapy, for example. The authors comment on "the shift from the

[26] Sullivan, *Psychology and Pedagogy*, 33.

[27] Spinelli, *The Mirror and the Hammer*, 170.

[28] Jeffrey Rubin, "Psychoanalysis is Self-Centered" in *Soul on the Couch: Spirituality, Religion and Morality in Contemporary Psychoanalysis*, eds. Charles Spezzano and Gerald J. Gargiulo (Hillsdale NJ: Analytic Press, 1997) 82.

[29] Isaac Prilleltensky, "Bridging Agency, Theory and Action: Critical Links in Critical Psychology" in *Critical Psychology: Voices for Change*, ed. Tod Sloan (New York: St. Martin's Press, 2000) 73.

sociability and community-centeredness of the pre-modern family to the privatized modern family."[30] Further, this shift to an "inward focus has removed the family from its role as an integral part of the larger moral ecology tying the individual to community, church and nation and placed it at the core of the private sphere, whose aim is not to link individuals to the public world but to avoid it as far as possible."[31] These pervasive notions, Ian Parker adds, "structure who we have become through contemporary psychological culture."[32]

For all its pointed criticism of psychology, critical psychology is not without its own problems. First, it contains a vast diversity in theoretical approach. That diversity naturally lends itself to many conflicting and contradictory positions. Second, those within critical psychology who advocate a postmodern deconstruction of the self and push psychology toward sociology do so with an equally unreflective embrace of social constructionism to counter what proponents see as the Western idealization of individualism. Third, there are equally passionate voices within critical psychology who are appealing to a universal and somewhat ethically charged criterion for care, responsibility, community, and justice within the realm of individual health and well-being.

Critical psychology, on the one hand, has raised serious criticism of psychology's claim to be a natural scientific methodology rather than a set of assumptions and beliefs that are historically and culturally situated. Psychology, as such, the critics charge, is not a neutral enterprise; theorists and therapists are not and cannot be neutral. As Prilleltensky and Nelson point out, we should not believe that "research is neutral, that interventions are not affected by politics, and that we are just healers."[33] What we define as "well-being," for example, is fraught with cultural and political implications. An individual's well-being, as Prilleltensky and Nelson argue, is "predicated on the well being of the family, which in turn is

---

[30] Frank C. Richardson, Blaine J. Fowers, and Charles B. Guignon. *Re-envisioning Psychology: Moral Dimensions of Theory and Practice* (San Francisco: Jossey-Bass Publishers, 1999) 75.

[31] Ibid.

[32] Ian Parker, "Critical Psychology: Excitement and Danger," *The International Journal of Critical Psychology* 1/1 (2001): 127.

[33] Prilleltensky and Nelson, *Doing Psychology Critically*, 6.

predicated on the well being of the community."[34] And Parker suggests that "the discipline of psychology does not only rest in the mechanics of laboratory experimentation but also just as firmly in the lures of humanism [and] the personal incarnation for each of us...."[35]

Thus, the vast territory of critical psychology also has divisions in its critique of psychology's mandate. Critics argue that the idealization of the self and self-actualization diminish social and ethical bonds. Yet critics of psychology also argue that the dependence on scientific paradigms and the resultant dependence on statistical generalities are inadequate in capturing the uniqueness of individual lives, if not the essence of human phenomena. This latter argument suggests that being human and understanding human nature is complex and perhaps cannot be both generalized and manipulated. This makes critical psychology difficult to gauge in terms of its usefulness or impact.

A common thread emerging from critical psychology does raise philosophical questions about the kind of world we live in and what our "individual" response should be. Criticism aimed at psychology's emphasis on the individual has led to suggestions that psychology should acknow-ledge its part in social justice, social cohesion, and altruistic and destructive expressions of human endeavor. Suggestions that "psychotherapeutic concern for the meaning of symptoms replaces questions about meaning or ultimate concern,"[36] "that psychoanalysis [in particular] seems to underestimate human possibility,"[37] and that the "ambiguities and dilemmas of daily life...provide a better understanding of human experience and action"[38] reveal once again a strong moral tenor within the divergent voices of critical psychology. Psychological inquiries that open the door to ultimate concern, the ambiguities of life and human possibility (which include meanings, values, and faith) also open psychology to multidisciplinary responses and collaborations. For those familiar with the work of Viktor Frankl and Paul Tillich, this kind of

---

[34] Ibid., 10.

[35] Ibid., 127.

[36] Rubin, "Psychoanalysis," 81.

[37] Ibid., 86.

[38] Ernest Schraube, "Reflecting on Who We Are in a Technical World" in *Critical Psychology: Voices for Change*, ed. Tod Sloan (New York: St. Martin's Press, 2000) 46.

collaboration and multidisciplinary response is a continuation of debate and analysis on the meaning of psychological health and well-being. Perhaps these voices from the past can contribute to the historical, religious, philosophical, and ethical foundations of contemporary theory such as critical psychology.

Viktor Frankl and Paul Tillich: Foreshadowing Critical Psychology

Viktor Frankl and Paul Tillich each believed that psychology had to accept the ambiguous and paradoxical character of human existence. As we saw in chapter 3, Frankl suggested that every psychological theory has a specific philosophy of human nature at its foundation. Every psychological theory contains some concept of what it is to be human and what constitutes psychological growth, development, and well-being. Frankl's belief that psychological theories offered multiple interpretations of what it was to be human did not always find receptive audiences in the mid- to late twentieth century when the discipline of psychology emphasized and sought scientific certainty and legitimacy. Ironically, contemporary voices within critical psychology have discovered the idea of multiple interpretations. Anderson comments:

> Postmodern psychologies are not in search of true psychological knowledge or psychological knowledge as definitive reality, but, rather, invite the multiple interpretations of any psychological phenomenon. This position on multiplicity moves knowledge away from something that is fixed to something that is alive, and in and through the interchanges of the multiple viewpoints, something new and novel emerges specific to the participants and their local situations and circumstances. Thus the certainty and predictability of psychological knowledge goes by the wayside.[39]

Frankl had similarly acknowledged that this "certainty and predictability," so favored by a discipline that aimed to be a science, manifested itself in what he called the foundational "concept of man," which essentially preceded theory. These foundational philosophies motivated and framed

---

[39] Harlene Anderson, "Reflections on the Appeals and the Challenges of Postmodern Psychologies, Societal Practice, and Political Life" in *Postmodern Psychologies, Societal Practice and Political Life*, eds. Lois Holzman and John Morss, (New York: Routledge, 2000) 202.

our psychological enquiries, and these, in turn, influenced psychological studies and subsequent analysis. What is rarely addressed is the extent to which these foundational philosophies also contain our hopes and faith about who we are and what we are capable of. Tillich expressed a similar sentiment when he wrote, "It is not always easy to distinguish the element of faith from the element of scientific hypothesis in a psychological assertion."[40] Tillich suggests that psychological theory is as much influenced by our hopes and beliefs about human nature and by how we creatively imagine the possibilities of human development and behavior as it is by scientific interpretations about what it is to be human.

Frankl, as we saw, argued that human beings were spiritual beings. We are spiritual beings because of our human capacity to experience the world, to contemplate and construct what is meaningful and valuable, to live in relationship, and to take in the world on deep experiential and emotive levels. Human life is marked by what Frankl termed our self-transcendence, our continuous movement outward beyond our individuality toward something or someone. Self-transcendence defies the scientific parameters and predictability of human behavior by suggesting an open-ended and continuous movement and striving beyond our present situation. The dynamic of relationship, dialogue, creativity, experience, and transcendence that characterizes human life is what marks us as spiritual beings.

One of the aims of Frankl's Logotherapy as a therapeutic practice was (and is) to help the individual become conscious of his or her responsibility. Frankl defined responsibility as a response-in-action. This was the ethical imperative of all human beings, an obligation to constantly reach out toward others, to be constantly engaged with others, and to be open to others. This implied a human striving on an ethical level to meet another individual in fellowship. Our existence points both inward and outward. To live humanely and, therefore, ethically is to respond to the world and participate in the world beyond our individuality. Frankl linked this specific ethical goal with positive psychological development, if not psychological health itself. Responsibility was shifted from a strictly individual accountability to a relational and shared response to the world. Individual responsibility was inextricably tied to the developments within

---

[40] Paul Tillich, *Dynamics of Faith* (New York: Harper & Row, 1957) 84–85.

culture. As we saw in chapter 3, the value of the individual was not only linked to but, in fact, dependent upon community. Conversely, the health and welfare of community was of little value without the uniqueness and diversity of the individuals who composed it. The ethical challenge for psychology was, and remains still, the acceptance and integration of this paradox.

Paul Tillich grappled with a similar paradox of individualism and universalism, between the dignity of an individual's life and the public good. Tillich linked what he termed the "courage to be as oneself" and "the courage to be a part." "The courage to be as oneself" is the "affirmation of the self as the self; that is of a separated, self-centered, individualized, incomparable, free, self-determining self."[41] Yet individuality is concurrently situated within a myriad of contexts, so the "courage to be a part" "points to the fact that self-affirmation necessarily includes the affirmation of oneself as participant."[42] A psychological and ethical principle also lies at the foundation of Tillich's concept of the "courage to be a part." Tillich suggested that it is the individual's participation in the "creative activities of society"[43] that confronts anxiety and reduces its debilitating effects. Much like Frankl, Tillich believed psychological health and development at both the individual and cultural level was an embodiment of two seemingly contradictory activities: actualizing one's unique potentials while being an integrated member of society.

Tillich ties this in with his concept of faith as ultimate concern. He saw faith as an inherently human characteristic. Faith was the acceptance of the contingencies and multiple dimensions of human life. Faith transcended both rational and non-rational aspects of human expression. Faith was cognitive and emotive, certain and uncertain, cast with risk and doubt. While some within critical psychology argue that an erosion of "truths" and "meaningfulness" in modern times ultimately affects our sense of self, community, and, by implication, faith, Tillich argued that faith did not mean "truth" but, rather, to be ultimately concerned. Such a definition of faith implies that the individual is continually in relation, is actively engaged with the world, concerned and responsible for its inhabitants, and

---

[41] Paul Tillich, *The Courage to Be* (New Haven CT: Yale University Press, 1980) 86.

[42] Ibid., 89.

[43] Ibid., 111.

open to the possibility of change. To be ultimately concerned is an individual response, one that emerges from a unique and centered self, but a response anchored in and motivated by the deepest questions about our existence, which are answered, in part, by our commitment to the world through collaboration and responsibility. To be ultimately concerned, according to Tillich, is an "act of the total personality...the most centered act of the human mind."[44] In Tillich's terms, it is an act of faith. Faith entails motivation toward dialogue, toward relationship, and toward community. It implies possibility. It involves a relationship between "the one who is concerned and his concern."[45]

Ultimate concern is not merely subjective motivation or belief, it is directed and has context. Tillich states, "[S]ince faith leads to action and action presupposes community, the state of ultimate concern is actual only within a community of action."[46] To be ultimately concerned, to have faith, involves a "centered self" freely responding, deciding, and simultaneously participating in relationship. Ultimate concern describes our human ability to have faith, to trust, to receive, and to grow. It also implies constructed, shared, and perpetuated values. It implies moral obligations and responsibilities, whether we always act morally or not, whether we act in a just fashion in every encounter or not. "The moral imperative," Tillich states, "is the command to become what one potentially is, a person within a community of persons."[47] Extended to ideas of psychological health and development, the potential that resides within each unique individual both depends upon and shapes the potential that resides within a community of persons. Ultimate concern embodies this relationship or concurrent dependency. "Faith," Tillich states, "is not a matter of the mind in isolation, or of the soul in contrast to mind and body, or of the body, but is the centered movement of the whole personality toward something of ultimate meaning and significance."[48]

Two additional quotes from Anderson, taken from a recent collection of essays on critical psychology, are worth examining as they are, once again, reminiscent of Frankl's and Tillich's thematic emphasis. In the first

---

[44] Tillich, *Dynamics*, 4.

[45] Ibid., 9.

[46] Ibid., 117.

[47] Paul Tillich, *Morality and Beyond* (New York: Harper & Row, 1966) 19.

[48] Tillich, *Dynamics*, 106.

example, Anderson discusses "postmodernism's attempt to promote dialogue, value difference, entertain uncertainty, and self-critique—widening our possibilities—rather than to promote monologue, sameness, and certainty—narrowing our possibilities."[49] As I read this sentence, I began substituting Tillich's language: "[T]o promote dialogue" became Tillich's idea of encounter, the act of "coming from both sides, of meeting in a common situation, of participation in this situation by becoming part of it."[50] The phrase "value difference" became the uniqueness and dignity of individual life. The phrase "entertain uncertainty" became Tillich's notion of the ambiguity of life. Human existence, according to Tillich, was ambiguous at every moment. The phrase "widening our possibilities" became Tillich's moral imperative that actualizing our potentialities was, once again, "the command to become what one potentially is, a person within a community of persons."[51]

In the second example, Anderson refers to postmodern concepts stating, "An identifiable family trait within this diversity is the distinction that language and knowledge are relational and generative. That is, reality—the meanings that we give to the events, experiences, people, and things in our lives—is communally constructed and inherently susceptible to transformation."[52] I immediately thought of Frankl's idea that we continually search for and construct meaning within our lives. The search for meaning (the will to meaning) implies a relational and contextual interdependence between the individual and the world around him or her, thereby suggesting the communal construction of meanings. We are engaged simultaneously as individuals and as community in a continuous process of discovering meaning, solidifying those meanings through decision, action, and creativity, and then beginning the process anew. The idea that meanings, both individual and collective, are susceptible to transformation fits Frankl's oft-repeated phrase that meanings change from moment to moment and from hour to hour.

As we have seen, critical psychology encompasses a wide theoretical terrain. It incorporates a varied spectrum of approaches to psychology, both

---

[49] Anderson, "Reflections on Appeals," 202.

[50] Paul Tillich, *The Spiritual Situation in Our Technical Society*, ed. J. Mark Thomas (Macon GA: Mercer University Press, 1998) 66.

[51] Tillich, *Morality and Beyond*, 202.

[52] Anderson, "Reflections on Appeals," 202.

from within the discipline and from without. Much of the debate within critical psychology centers on issues of individuality and community, or, put another way, on issues of particularity versus universality. While some debate focuses on the scientific universalism of psychological theory to the detriment of individual expression and uniqueness, others debate the cultural, religious, and political dangers of universalism and posit, if not an advocacy of individualism, certainly an advocacy of particularity and uniqueness.

In the previous chapters, we saw illustrations of several historical debates and dialogues that attempted to bridge but ultimately accept these paradoxes. Mental health and well-being for theologians and psychologists alike meant transcending strict theory or dogma and collaboratively focusing attention, expertise, faith, and hope on an appeal to the common good, to social justice, and peaceful coexistence. As we saw in chapter 3, Frankl was passionately vocal that psychological theory should view the individual as more than mere organism, more than a social construction. It was imperative that the value of the individual, Frankl stressed, be upheld considering the very real possibility of human extinction. Frankl's views resonate today as we in the West struggle to balance our devotion to individual expression while recognizing the need for community and partnership. These sentiments also resonate with current debates within critical psychology. Frankl's contention that Logotherapy attempts to answer the psychotherapeutic needs of our time reveals his clear belief—similar to that of critical psychology—that psychological theory is historically and culturally situated. The implicit assumptions and underlying philosophy of any given theory emerge from a particular historical point and so are laden with myriad cultural contexts. Frankl is also saying something about the scientism pervading psychological theory and practice through the twentieth century. His statement clearly rejects a universal scientific model to analyze human beings, but the statement also calls on a universal response that is morally and ethically situated in community, care, and compassion. Frankl's statement contends that individual expression is particular, unique, and of value while simultaneously pointing to an implicit message of social interconnectedness and responsibility.

Paul Tillich weighed these same ambiguities and realities of human existence. As a theologian and religious philosopher, Tillich engaged in psychological discourse to enrich his thinking. It has been suggested that Tillich's theology was political.[53] I believe this to be true, and I believe Tillich's psychology was also greatly politicized. I would like to cite the following two examples. In a section entitled "Ambiguities of Humanism" in volume 3 of *Systematic Theology*, Tillich debates the possibility that a culture could exist in which individual potentials could be fully realized. Leaving aside Tillich's argument that human beings are finite beings, thereby argumentatively incapable of fully actualizing their potentialities, Tillich offers the following statement: "[B]ut even worse, the human condition always excludes—whether under aristocratic or democratic systems—the vast majority of human beings from the higher grades of cultural form and educational depth."[54] This statement is particularly interesting in light of critical psychology's claim that psychological theory and therapy have entrenched themselves within a very particular Western socioeconomic context. Several critiques of psychology from this angle have questioned the universality of such notions as self-actualization and the actualization of potentials without reference to the "facts" or the context of an individual's life, and whether theoretical assumptions about how one self-actualizes can really be salient across differing economic realities. Transposed onto current debates, Tillich's statement reminds us who is actually served by psychology and whether or not psychology is sufficiently self-aware of the politicized ideologies and assumptions it conveys about who we are and how we are to develop "normal" and fulfilling lives.

The second illustration of Tillich's political psychology comes from a radio address he broadcast from the United States to Germany during the Second World War. From a broadcast entitled "Justice and Humanity," Tillich states,

> Your rights are the acknowledgment that you are a person, that you have dignity that is inviolable, that you are a uniquely irreplaceable self. They are the acknowledgment that you are human. Deprival of justice is deprival of humanity. Human dignity is one with its justice. Without dignity, representatives of the German people have dispensed with their

---

[53] *Against the Third Reich: Paul Tillich's Wartime Radio Broadcasts into Nazi Germany*, eds. Ronald H. Stone and Matthew Lon Weaver (Louisville KY: Westminster John Knox Press, 1998) 6.

[54] Paul Tillich, *Systematic Theology*, vol. 3 (Chicago: University of Chicago Press, 1967) 86.

> rights and, with that, have surrendered the dignity of the nation and every single individual. Reclaim your rights again, German people, and with it yourselves![55]

Although the quotation conveys the understandable emotions of the time in relation to the audience to whom it was directed, it also reveals the nuanced, ambiguous, and difficult debate surrounding the dignity and uniqueness of individual expression, the links between individual and collective responsibility, the idealism of individuality and community, individual and communal faith and hope. Within the historical and political context of this speech, Tillich conveys idealism, hope, faith, and a moral imperative that suggests a possible path through the debate. Such a path would address individuality, community, individual responsibility, and collective social justice. Such a path would navigate the relationship between reality and possibility.

The relationship between reality and possibility conveyed in so much of what Frankl and Tillich wrote posits an awareness and responsibility in partnership with faith and hope. The ethical imperative to become a person in a community of persons, as Frankl and Tillich similarly express, suggests self-awareness and response, reflection and decision, a dialogue with and relationship to the world around us. It requires us to constantly juggle and, therefore, debate the desire for equality, peace, and the freedom of individual as well as community or cultural expression. How do we account for an individual's ability to believe, to have unwavering faith, to have one's faith shattered, to create, to dream, to destroy, to imagine, to love, to hate, to hope, to despair? How do we account for an individual's ability to construct meaningful ways of living and experiencing? When an individual in therapy describes experiences of meaninglessness, of love, anger, or joy, do these experiences reside solely within the realm of psychology when psychological theory is itself ambiguous and changing? How do we account for the fact that these same individual experiences and expressions are simultaneously culturally situated and are manifested collectively in the growth, development, faith, destruction, values, and social justice of nations, groups, or cultures?

Postmodern theories such as critical psychology are contributing greatly to how we see the discipline of psychology and remind us of the

---

[55] *Against the Third Reich*, eds. Stone and Weaver , 27.

importance of questioning the aim and purpose of psychological theory and therapy. Is there a discernable centered self, a self who expresses identifiable experience uniquely separate from social, historical, and political contexts? Is therapy engaged in the purely subjective experiences of the client or is it a tangled discourse of subjective experience, feelings, meanings, and beliefs, all of which influence and are influenced by social, political, historical, religious, and ethical contexts? This also raises the question regarding the extent to which psychology should in fact be engaged in these discussions. If, as critics charge, psychology perpetuates a strong Westernized vision of individualism and excludes notions of relation and community well-being from its psychological categorizations, we come back to a recurring question of whether psychology excludes itself from social responsibility and why. If, as critics charge, psychology should be engaged ethically in the well-being of a community, does critical psychology, for example, assume that psychology should at some level be facilitating socially aware and socially engaged citizens? Is a therapist, in fact, engaged in much broader issues when clients expresses their belief systems, when they express what is meaningful and valuable, when they situate their experiences simultaneously with the experiences of family, work, community, and broader social contexts? These contexts themselves are also continually shifting and changing in harmony and at odds with the changes and shifts in what constitutes "self." Is an "individual" in therapy expressing unique experiences and unique responses to these contexts? These recurring questions also remind us that current debates have much to gain from those who have previously explored psychology's place within our culture.

Tillich believed that all dimensions and expressions of culture co-existed and influenced one another. His theological and philosophical writings embraced a relationship and dialogue with psychology, sociology, anthropology, science, the arts, history, and politics. Although Tillich had a keen interest in psychology and integrated psychological terminology into many of his ideas, he was critical of the increasing influence and implication of the natural sciences on psychology. Tillich stated, "It is the temptation of science to transform everything encountered, including man, into an object that is nothing other than an object. Obviously, every scientific inquiry has an object opposite the inquiring subject. And the more deprived a being is of subjectivity, namely, spontaneous reactions, the more precisely can it be analyzed."[56] Tillich suggested that "under these pressures, man can hardly escape the fate of becoming a thing among things he produces, a bundle of conditioned reflexes without a free, deciding and responsible self."[57]

We recall in a paper given to the New York Psychology Group[58] in 1943, quoted in chapter 2, in which Tillich described the "eccentricity of the human mind," which he claimed made it impossible to formulate a "closed system" in relation to being.[59] In many respects, Tillich had a particular notion of the self far closer to that of the critical psychologists than to that of conventional or mainstream psychology. For Tillich, a person was a multidimensional unity that required a multidimensional response,[60] not at all isolated and divorced from the world. Tillich described an individual's growth as contingent upon relationship with others. He stated, "A person becomes a person in the encounter with other persons, and in no other way."[61] As a result, human existence should be seen as an open and relational process. Yet Tillich believed there was a "centered self" that was capable of a "centered reaction [which] goes through deliberation and decision."[62] Individual deliberation and decision begins by encountering, taking in, reacting to, and then moving out toward encounter again through participation and response. "Only [man]," Tillich wrote, "has a completely centered self and a structured universe to which he belongs and at which he is able to look at the same time."[63] The "centered self" is a unique and individual expression or reaction. A decision, a glimpse of possibility, our imagination, the ability to reflect on our creative

---

[56] Tillich, *Spiritual Situation*, 81.

[57] Ibid., 45.

[58] The New York Psychology Group of the National Council on Religion and Higher Education, 1941–1945, hereafter cited as NYPG. From the collection of Prof. Allison Stokes of Ithaca College, New York.

[59] Paul Tillich, New York Psychology Group (NYPG), 19 May 1943.

[60] Paul Tillich, "The Meaning of Health" in *The Meaning of Health: Essays in Existentialism, Psychoanalysis and Religion*, ed. Perry LeFevre (Chicago: Exploration Press, 1984) 167.

[61] Paul Tillich, "Existentialism and Psychotherapy," in *The Meaning of Health*, 163.

[62] *Paul Tillich in Conversation: Psychotherapy, Religion, Culture, History and Psychology*, ed. James B. Ashbrook (Bristol IN: Wyndham Hall Press, 1988) 136.

[63] Paul Tillich, *Systematic Theology*, vol. 2 (Chicago: University of Chicago Press, 1967) 60.

endeavors—all of these are uniquely human capabilities that are expressed individually through the unity of psychic, physical, and spiritual dimensions. Tillich asks us to accept the paradox that we are individually free to some extent and that such possibility also has social reference and relation. Possibility points to a capability of transcending immediate concrete situations. This implies both individual and cultural transcendence. To transcend is to move beyond the immediate toward relationship, toward dialogue. Human life, therefore, is marked both by its possibility and the implied ethical responsibility that exists in encounter.

Echoing Tillich's views, albeit unknowingly, some voices in critical psychology express a clear ethical direction for psychology. The direction psychology must take, according to Prilleltensky, for example, is the balance between the individual and the collective. The psychological aim of "wellness" must be both personal and collective. Prilleltensky states, "The liberation of the self is intimately connected to the liberation of the other. The personal well-being of the individual is predicated on the availability of communal resources such as health and safety. Caring only about individual clients or friends or relatives is insufficient to secure a caring society."[64] Community and individual "wellness" do need to be seen side by side, as each is in constant interplay with the other. In addition, a critical approach to psychology needs to continually raise the large and ambiguous questions, such as what constitutes "wellness" and what are the implications of exposing clear moral directives within the discipline of psychology. We need to ask, "Don't we need to know under what circumstances caring and compassion and fairness are likely to be upheld?"[65]

It is fascinating to see questions of care, individual and community health, and well-being continually reemerge. These questions remain with us, and they remind us that we are continually caught between our aspirations for universal answers and the ambiguous realities that challenge and confront us at each moment. Much like the discussions held during New York Psychology Group meetings, in which members asked how compassion, justice, and the care for others could be universally valued and upheld, Prilleltensky similarly asks whether we can truly know what these "circumstances" are that might lead to a communally shared ethic of care.

---

[64] Isaac Prilleltensky, "Emancipation, Epistemology, and Engagement: Challenges for Critical Psychology" in *The Journal for Critical Psychology*, 107.

[65] Ibid., 108.

What remains ambiguous and elusive is the continually shifting contexts that these circumstances are dependent upon. Does Prilleltensky's valid and important question not also raise the question of universal values, that is, those values shared by all human beings simply because we are human, with a faith in humanity, so that caring, compassion, and fairness are indeed upheld over time and across shifting contexts and circumstances? This kind of enquiry emerging from critical psychology resonates with theological and psychological dialogues from the past, which sounded urgent appeals for social justice.

Certainly one can argue that Tillich's concept of ultimate concern, for example, posits a Christian expression and moral directive that points to a universal faith in humanity, a faith that transcends both individuality and the particularities of community. Yet one also can argue that critical psychology, even in its critique of psychology's aim and purpose, advocates some form of ultimate concern for the welfare of all. Again, we are left with those areas that have yet to be fully reflected upon, the extent to which even secular postmodern critique harbors Judeo-Christian ethical foundations. As we recall, members of the New York Psychology Group wondered in June 1943 whether a concept advocating the unity of humankind could develop from an ideology into a reality.[66] We still grapple with these questions.

Conclusion

In the previous three chapters, we explored several historical voices that foreshadowed much of critical psychology, indeed much of contemporary psychological debate. Similar questions continue to be raised about what psychology does, who it serves, and whether it adequately addresses what it is to be human. Current questions being asked by critical psychology focus on the ambiguity that emerges in psychological theory and therapy when they confront the cultural, religious, ethical, economic, and political contexts that both influence theory and are influenced by psychological paradigms. Tillich's and Frankl's dialogue between theology and psychology provides a possible bridge and points of connection amidst this ambiguity.

If human existence is, as Tillich describes, multidimensional, then the response must necessarily be wide and varied. The relationship between

---

[66] Members Discussion, NYPG, 4 June 1943.

reality and possibility conveyed in so much of what both Frankl and Tillich wrote posits an awareness and responsibility in partnership with faith and hope. Tillich's idea that the individual becomes (or develops) within a continuous, reciprocal, and mutual relationship between self and world, between self and "other," is a precursor to critical psychology's argument that psychology as a discipline has stressed a specific and static concept of the individual, ignoring the social, political, historical, and religious contexts that contribute to "becoming." Further, Tillich's concept of ultimate concern implies an ethical and responsive dialogue between self and world. Similarly, contemporary therapists and theorists in psychology who are attempting to discuss the ethical overlays of individual and community growth, development, and well-being have much to gain from historical interdisciplinary dialogue and those who have been concerned by many of the same things. That many of the same questions reemerge indicates similar, continuing aspirations and hope about human development.

Where might these questions and debates, both historical and contemporary, lead, in terms of therapy itself, for example? As we saw at the beginning of the chapter, many contemporary therapists have questioned psychotherapeutic traditions that essentially ignore a client's experiences and expressions of faith, hope, commitment to others, and commitment to the world. Tillich stated that the "interdependence of [man] and [man] in the process of becoming human is a judgment against a psychotherapeutic me-thod in which the patient is a mere object for the analyst as subject."[67] Here, too, Tillich was foreshadowing much of the scrutiny of therapy by critical psychology, in particular the assumed neutrality and objectivity of the therapist toward his or her client. Since Frankl believed that a patient had "the right to demand that the ideas [he] advances be treated on the philo-sophical level," we might expand upon this concept to present day. It could be said that today's patient has the right to demand that the ideas he or she advances be treated in light of the wide and varied contextual levels in which the individual lives and that the therapist be open to such dialogue.

We now turn to the contemporary theory of existential analysis, a possible answer to Hans Hofmann's search for a psychological theory that embodied the "real human factor."

[67] Tillich, "Existentialism," 163.

"In the Midst of This World I Discover Myself Unmistakably":[1] Alfried Längle's Theory of Existential Analysis

> In all the ruin there remains the potentiality of [man himself]. Only the individual, whether in public or private, can provide the spark for the rebuilding of real community, which may again breathe a soul into the technological world of industry.... It is not true that the individual has disappeared.... Yet he needs others to be able to remain [himself].[2]

Introduction

Human life is simultaneously singular and communal, unique and shared. This chapter's opening quotation, written by Karl Jaspers in 1959, remains powerfully pertinent today and resonates with Alfried Längle's[3]

---

[1] Alfried Längle, "The Search for Meaning in Life and the Existential Fundamental Motivations," *International Journal of Existential Psychology & Psychotherapy* 1/1 (July 2004): 34.

[2] Karl Jaspers, "The Individual and Mass Society" in *Religion and Culture: Essays in Honor of Paul Tillich*, ed. Walter Leibrecht (New York: Harper & Brothers, 1959) 43.

[3] Dr. Alfried Längle, M.D., Ph.D., is an analyst in private practice in Vienna, Austria. He is founder and president of the International Society for Logotherapy and Existential Analysis. Dr. Längle worked with Viktor Frankl for 10 years and developed the theory of Existential Analysis during that time. He teaches frequently at universities in Austria, South America, and Moscow. He gives frequent lectures and conducts training seminars in Existential Analysis throughout many European countries, in addition to Australia, Canada, and the United States. This chapter is based on my knowledge of Existential Analysis from lectures, seminars, and conference workshops Dr. Längle conducted and which I attended in Vancouver, British Columbia, between 2002 and 2005; regular personal correspondence with Dr. Längle from 2002 to the present; meetings with Dr.Längle in Vienna, Austria, in May 2003 and again in May of 2004; and, finally, several translated articles on Existential Analysis in which Dr. Längle kindly asked for my editorial assistance. I am indebted to his generosity, mentorship, and support of my interests and work based on his theory.

contemporary theory of existential psychotherapy. The potential for individual and cultural transformation, Jaspers states, lies within a shared commitment that values the dignity and uniqueness of the individual while acknowledging that human life is also necessarily dependent and interconnected. Längle's theory of existential analysis[4] is a contemporary argument for this interdependence of self and world. Human existence, Längle states, is fundamentally "dialogical."

The purpose of this chapter is to focus on Längle's theory and therapy of existential psychotherapy as an illustration of the continuing and enduring themes about what makes us truly human and what it means to live a psychologically healthy life. In order to illustrate this, the chapter will focus on four points. First, we begin by questioning our assumptions of what therapy should provide. The Western world has become increasingly saturated with therapy culture, and this has had a profound impact on how we see ourselves and how we gauge our lives. Second, we give a brief overview of existential analysis, including its emphasis on the dialogical nature of human existence. Third, we continue with an outline of what Längle calls the four fundamental existential motivations. And finally, we conclude with a dialogue between Paul Tillich and existential analysis. Much of the debate and belief about human potential contained in the historical dialogues we have examined in the previous chapters—and that transcend the disciplinary boundaries of psychology and theology—continues in some quarters of contemporary psychological theory. Historical dialogues remain an untapped resource for postmodern theory, particularly those dialogues that question the purpose of psychology as well as our capabilities and responsibilities as human beings, that plea for a humane approach to care, and that define the constituents of psychological health and notions of well-being. Existential analysis, by contrast, is theoretically grounded in dialogue and is, as a result, open to interdisciplinary collaboration. Längle's theory of existential analysis provides a valuable bridge to such collaboration in the following ways. First, the "dialogical" encounter between therapist and client, fundamental to the therapeutic practice of existential analysis, exposes the depth and ambiguity of human encounter. Second, the focus on human encounter

---

[4] Existential Analysis is a psychotherapeutic method developed by Dr. Alfried Längle.

and dialogue opens the door to discussing and analyzing the ethical subtext contained in human potential and responsibility. These two points are strikingly similar to the issues raised in the historical dialogues between psychologists and theologians whose aim was to foster an ethically deeper and more responsive approach to both the study and care of human beings. Erich Fromm once wrote, "Psychology can show us what [man] is not. It cannot tell us what [man], each one of us, is. The soul of [man], the unique core of each individual, can never be grasped and described adequately...the legitimate aim of psychology thus is the negative, the removal of distortions and illusions, not the positive, the full and complete knowledge of a human being."[5] Längle's theory of existential analysis may be one contemporary psychotherapeutic approach that focuses on exposing the positive potentials and possibilities that lie within the enduring mystery of human existence.

We saw in the previous chapter how some postmodern debate within critical psychology continues to weigh individuality against the social world. Is there such a thing as "I," separate and discernible from social referents? Can psychology, the critics suggest, uphold a notion of the self that is distinguishable from the influence of cultural, political, or economic constructions? Is our notion of the individual self merely a social construction? Those engaged in critical psychology, for example, are attempting to reconceptualize psychological theory by scrutinizing its fundamental assumptions and biases. By doing so, the question arises as to psychology's elevation of the self and perpetuation of individuality distinctly separate from the myriad contexts in which the self resides, contributes to, and is influenced by. We also saw that despite the important issues and questions critical psychology has raised for the discipline itself, some within critical psychology fall prey to simply choosing the other end of the spectrum and prioritizing social constructionist theory, or sociology itself, to analyze human existence. Once again, raising legitimate concerns about psychology's aim and purpose is necessary and fruitful, but deconstructing psychology's human subject negates any possibility of dialogue or transcending theoretically constructed opposites, individuality and community. Situating human existence within

[5] Erich Fromm, "The Limitations and Dangers of Psychology," in *Religion and Culture: Essays in Honor of Paul Tillich*, ed. Walter Leibrecht (New York: Harper & Brothers, 1959) 33.

an interrelational foundation opens a path to dialogue, which, in turn, enables us to discuss and analyze individual and community potential with equal commitment.

Existential analysis does not deconstruct or negate a concept of individuality; rather, this contemporary therapeutic approach bridges the uniqueness and dignity of individual existence with the social world. There is, according to existential analysis, a discernible and unique self simultaneously embedded in the social world. Jaspers's comment at the beginning of this chapter reminds us of the need to value individual life sufficiently in order to enable each of us to take on what Tillich saw as our moral obligation: to become a person within a community of persons. This entails our creative potential, "the spark" that Jaspers refers to, being relationally directed outward into the world. As we saw at the beginning of chapter 5, some contemporary therapists have resisted the postmodern urge to render individuality a mere social construction and are paying attention to the words, stories, actions, and feelings of their clients as potentially ethically meaningful relationships and dialogues with the world. Many contemporary therapists are devoting their attention to preserving the potentiality that exists in the individual "spark" and to ask how our preservation of humanity within psychological theory and therapy might transcend outward into an ethic of goodwill and community. At the 2004 meetings of the International Network on Personal Meaning, Paul Wong commented upon what an existential psychotherapy could mean for the twenty-first century. Acknowledging the range of theoretical contributors to the field of existential psychology, Wong narrowed in on some general characteristics when he stated, "Existential psychology needs to become the practical psychology of everyday living.... [S]hifting through the colliding narratives and contradicting 'facts,' existential psychology seeks to address fundamental questions relevant to the survival of humanity and the well-being of every individual."[6]

What Should Therapy Provide?

We might extend Erich Fromm's comment about what psychology can or cannot show us and ask, What do we assume therapy should provide? Within the vast array of psychological theories and

---

[6] Paul Wong, "Existential Psychology for the 21st Century," *International Journal of Existential Psychology & Psychotherapy* 1/1 (July 2004): 1.

psychotherapies available, those who provide therapy and those who seek it have assumptions about what therapy is and what it should provide. Underneath these initial views lie further assumptions about what constitutes mental health, well-being, and a fulfilling existence. What criteria do therapists use to gauge the mental health and overall psychological well-being of their clients? Are these criteria based primarily on the theoretical framework the therapists work within? To what extent does a therapist assess another human being's psychological well-being and then convey alterations or adaptations for the client to follow in order to maximize an already elusive term like "well-being"? Similarly, what criteria does the client rely on to assess the state of his or her own mental health and/or sense of well-being? Is it subjective experience and self-knowledge alone? Is it an internalization of specific cultural assumptions and expectations about what constitutes a healthy or unhealthy, fulfilling or disruptive existence? Is the internalization of psychological beliefs about human nature assumed to be a reliable gauge of human expression and development? If one could clearly identify the criteria a client was relying upon, what would that person then expect of therapy and the therapist? Is therapy assumed to "help," and what would "help" be experienced as? Does therapy significantly alter or change an individual's life? Does therapy facilitate and guide or does it dictate what a psychologically healthy and fulfilling life is?

All of these questions and underlying assumptions are based on philosophical notions about human existence and development that lie at the foundation of every psychological theory, whether implicitly or explicitly acknowledged. What, for example, constitutes psychological health and what does it mean to be free from anxiety, neurosis, or psychic disorders? We assume psychological health and well-being means a "normal" process of living and development. But health and well-being are concepts influenced not only by cultural notions and definitions of what normal is and where "normalcy" falls on a continuum of mental health and disease, they also imply some notion of what life is like in the absence of psychological disorder. Are psychological theories aware, if not overt, in expressing what life or human existence *should* be in the absence of disorder? Could therapy be engaged in something far beyond the scientific paradigms that psychological theory favors? Are we not stepping into the realm of meanings, beliefs, values, and ethics? Are psychological theories, on some level, making statements not merely about our beliefs in human existence but also on our hopes about what we ought to do and should do? Do psychological and cultural constructions of "health" and "well-being" also point to ideas, if not ideals and hopes, of what it is to be a productive, responsible, and fulfilled citizen within the wider social arena? If such assumptions reside at the foundation of therapy, is therapy engaged in facilitating (if not producing) a responsible citizenry?

All of these questions are impossibly large, but as Hans Hofmann expressed at the beginning of the Harvard Project on Religion and Mental Health, they are always necessary to keep in mind, since they challenge and influence the scope and depth of our creative pursuits in these matters. Alfried Längle stated that the purpose of psychotherapy was to "help" an individual deal subjectively with "psychical and psychosocial problems and with suffering."[7] Further, and perhaps more significantly, psychotherapeutic help is based on *human* skills. Seeing psychology from a more human perspective, Längle contends that psychotherapy is not magic and that it has its limitations. "Its results," he stated, "may be no better than what the patient's own capacities, motivations and resources will allow."[8] This is an interesting statement because it raises the issue, yet again, about the internal power of the individual to decide, at some level, for or against what confronts him or her from the outside or external world. Simply put, despite all the scientific generalizations, equations, and theories about human nature, an individual can always take a different stand. Psychology should not promise a goal, Längle continues. Psychology's "horizon is smaller and more pragmatic; its aim is to help, or in cases of psychopathology, to cure."[9] Specifically, "psychotherapy is a craft [that] utilizes different tools that can help people deal more effectively with their problems and feelings...psychotherapy, therefore, may *open a way*,"[10] but it should refrain from dictating a specific direction or outcome for therapy. Erich Fromm provides an astute observation from the past in this regard:

> What happens so often in psychoanalytic treatment is that there is a silent agreement between therapist and patient which consists in the

[7] Alfried Längle, "Goals and Motivations in Existential Psychotherapy: The Four Fundamental Conditions for a Fulfilled Existence," 2. Can be found at http:www.laengle.info/al/al_pu_li.php?sprache=en; accessed 4 January 2003.

[8] Längle, "Goals and Motivations," 3.

[9] Ibid.

[10] Ibid.

> assumption that psychoanalysis is a method by which one can attain happiness and maturity, and yet avoid the [patient's own] leap...no amount or depth of psychological insight can ever take the place of the act, of the commitment, of the leap. It can lead to it, prepare it, make it possible—and this is the legitimate function of psychoanalytic work. But it must not try to be a substitute for the responsible act of commitment, an act without which no real change occurs in a human being.[11]

One could say there is a commitment within existential analysis to encourage the client to take that individual "leap."

Existential Analysis

The historical roots of existential analysis lie within Viktor Frankl's theory of Logotherapy. The foundational philosophy of existential analysis and its therapeutic emphasis on meaning and value owe much to Frankl's work. Längle has, however, taken this foundation and expanded on it greatly, thereby creating a far more extensive therapeutic approach.

Existential analysis is a useful theory in contemporary debates about the aim of therapy and the complexity of defining psychological "wellness." Existential analysis acknowledges the dialogue (as opposed to clinical interpretation) and engagement between therapist and client as open-ended and mutually transforming. Acknowledging therapy as a relational dialogue presumes mutual encounter, responsibility, reliance, faith, trust, and respect on both sides. The therapeutic encounter, as dialogue, is a reflection or mirror of human expression; a combination of fact and possibility. The therapeutic encounter involves the client's story of factual situations and realities, then moves to a reassessment or an emotional re-experiencing of the client's encounter with these same realities. This is followed by a reevaluation of those feelings and experiences in light of the present dialogue within therapy, the client's experience in the present moment, and the possibilities that emerge within this encounter. Therapy, therefore, from an existential psychotherapeutic perspective, is a spontaneous dialogue reflecting the experience of encounter between the client and therapist and the creative possibilities that emerge within this dialogue. These dialogues and the subjective experiences of both client and therapist are further shaped by cultural and social contexts, beliefs, meanings, and values. These

---

[11] Fromm, "Limitations and Dangers," 35–36.

contexts are embedded in the words, feelings, and actions of the client. Because existential analysis focuses on an open dialogue, the client's own language is exposed, and social, cultural, familial, and religious contexts become transparent. Further, because a therapist within an existential framework approaches the client with an attitude of dialogue and openness, these contexts are respected and validated. The client has the ability to dialogue using his or her own language (and one has to concede that this language will be complicated with the internalizations of psychological culture), and this, it is hoped, will also facilitate the client's ability to take that responsible leap toward change from his or her own reference points. Focusing on what is possible, the therapeutic encounter enables the client to grasp what is potentially creative and positive.

This kind of therapeutic encounter, however, begins with a specific approach, attitude, and stance toward human existence. Existential analysis is based on the interdependent or relational reality of human life. Individuality is not, as some would contend, non-existent. Individuality is real within relationship. Our individual responses, actions, and decisions are seen within the multiple contexts in which we exist. Therapy focuses on how we encounter the world, how we integrate the world around us, how we contribute to the world, how we respond to, accept, or challenge the facts of our existence, how we construct meaning, and, finally, on how we live creatively. All of these are seen within the contexts of both the subjective experience of clients and the world in which they live. Psychological growth, health, and development are contingent upon a client's participation, dialogue, engagement, and response to the world. It requires the individual to think, feel, react, and participate, both subjectively and beyond their subjectivity, by transcending, reaching beyond creatively through faith, hope, possibility, decision, and action. Once again, it is the "leap" Fromm alludes to, a leap toward the world that is precipitated by the client's acceptance and affirmation of who he or she is.

Längle's theory is a phenomenological approach and method of psychotherapy. In this particular theoretical context, phenomenological means that both therapist and patient come together with an attitude of openness, an attempt not to impose, manipulate, or control. A concerted effort is made to suspend judgment, interpretation, or theory in order to rely on "subjective intelligence, feeling and sensing."[12] This allows the phenomena or the experiences the individual has to "speak." Put another way, this approach literally allows our experiences to "speak for themselves."[13] Allowing our feelings, senses, and perceptions to speak in the moment without the imposition of interpretation offers a chance to glimpse and possibly understand what Längle describes as "the unique essence of an individual."[14] After many years of clinical and private practice, Längle believes that clients want to be understood and not interpreted.[15] Clients want their stories and experiences to be heard and empathetically received.

To summarize thus far, existential analysis integrates and attempts to mobilize an individual's subjective experience, freedom for decision, creativity, and action within and never divorced from the concurrent social contexts in which the individual is embedded. Understanding an individual's essential core is only possible through relationship and the dialogical act, a coordination of both inner and outer reality. The coordination of inner and outer reality, of possibility or potential, is dependent upon dialogue and decision. Let me illustrate using the first person. I, for example, am never free from the responsibility of decision or the attitudes I may or may not choose to adopt. Greater psychological understanding and growth on my part requires both my awareness of the dialogue I am embedded in and my unique responsibility. I must personally utilize my human ability to decide, choose, and act.

From an existential analytic perspective, human existence is viewed in the following ways: (a) Human existence is fundamentally dialogical. The individual and the world are inextricably linked and in constant dialogue. (b) Human existence is meaningful. A meaningful existence is shaped by freedom and responsibility (considered inherent human qualities in existential psychotherapies), yet individual freedom and responsibility are

---

[12] Alfried Längle, "Existential Fundamental Motivation" (paper presented at the 18th World Congress of Psychotherapy, Trondheim, Norway, 16 August 2002). Can be found at http:www.laengle.info/al/al_pu_li.php?sprache=en; accessed 4 January 2003.

[13] Ibid.

[14] Ibid.

[15] Personal notes taken during Längle's comments on an existential analytic approach to therapy. Weekend seminar on Existential Analysis held at Trinity Western University in Langley, British Columbia, 19–20 November 2004.

concurrently shaped by mutual dialogue between self and other, between self and world. (c) Human beings have drives, aims, goals, tasks, values, and purpose that they want to live out authentically. The aim of therapy is to help free an individual from the fixations, distortions, or traumas that influence his or her experiences or behavior and hinder the ability to engage fully in these purposeful tasks and goals. (d) Human existence is not static; it has movement and purpose. We have the ability to change things, we have the ability to experience what is of value and eliminate what is harmful. (e) The focus of existential analysis on subjective experience takes into account certain existential realities of human existence. For example, human beings suffer psychologically, physically, and spiritually. Human life has both tragic and infinitely fulfilling elements. Human beings are capable of both creative and destructive ventures. Human beings are capable of self-reflective thought, and this gives them the capacity to analyze their existence, placing their actions, thoughts, and feelings in context. The capacity for self-reflection enables us to make decisions and choose a course of action within these realities.

The aim of existential analysis is to assist a person toward authentic and responsible decisions with regard to life and the world. Existence is defined as a fully lived "whole" life, which is possible only in relationship and by being engaged with the world. Existential analysis retains the three-dimensional structure of the human psyche that we saw developed in Frankl's Logotherapy, that being the spiritual, psychological, and physical. The spiritual dimension corresponds with meanings, values, faith, justice, freedom, and responsibility. Längle has added four pillars of existence or cornerstones of reality: a) the world, which consists of facts, potentials, and supporting structures; b) life, which corresponds to our particular network of feelings and relationships; c) being oneself, existing as a unique and autonomous person; and d) the future, which we have the ability to shape and which incorporates meanings and values. It is Längle's contention that we have a continuous dialogue with each of these cornerstones.

Let us now take a closer look at what Längle means by "dialogical" and the implications of dialogue for our progress as human beings.

Human Existence as Dialogical

As stated, human existence, from an existential psychotherapeutic perspective, is "dialogical." By this, existential analysis refers to a fundamental characteristic of being human, namely, the active search and striving for dialogue, connection, and relation with others. Dialogical refers to our constant confrontation with other people, with the world, and even with ourselves. This continuous confrontation and encounter demands something of us. Again, let me illustrate using the first person. As a human being, I have the ability to access my unique freedom to evaluate situations as I encounter them. I assess the reality of a situation before me. I have the capacity to contemplate the possibilities or potential of any given moment or encounter I face. I have the freedom to decide in this moment what choice I will make, what stand I may take, or what kind of attitude I may adopt as I engage in the situation. This is, from an existential perspective, the continual challenge that confronts and distinguishes me as a human being. Längle states,

> The possibilities within this world point to our human potential: we shape our existence through these possibilities. "Existence" means having a chance to change things for the better, to experience what is of value and to avoid or eliminate what could be damaging or harmful. Possibilities provide us with directions to which we can orient ourselves. This is an essential orientation of human beings, not a superficial one. Being directed towards what is possible, what is yet to be fulfilled, what is waiting for us each in each and every situation corresponds perfectly to the essence of our spirit—a spirit that is looking out for participation, dialogue, creativity and possibility. We see the essential task of existence to be one of finding this correspondence between our potential for participation (for creativity, action and encounter) and what is possible, what is needed, what is undone, what we see and feel and understand to be waiting for us, despite the possibility of risk and error.[16]

Psychological health follows on such an approach. If my response to these encounters and confrontations is to be considered authentic, and, therefore, psychologically healthy, there must be a coordination of both inner and outer reality. My response must have my inner consent, a subjective affirmation at the experiential level that this is the right response. In addition, my response must also include a realistic assessment of the external world or outer reality.

---

[16] Alfried Längle, "The Search for Meaning in Life and the Existential Fundamental Motivations," *International Journal of Existential Psychology & Psychotherapy* 1/1 (July 2004): 29.

One can also initiate an ethical dialogue within this idea of encounter and confrontation. Every encounter challenges me in terms of my response. I may weigh what my response will be and evaluate my response and actions in terms of a personal moral stand or culturally shared ethics. I weigh what is possible or potential with what might be needed, demanded, or appropriate in a particular moment or situation. I weigh this against a backdrop of shifting realities, and I do this despite the fact that every decision I make is simultaneously cast in possible risk, doubt, or error. This is the existential paradox that further characterizes me as fundamentally human. Yet the existential analysis approach to psychotherapy is a decidedly optimistic approach of possibility in the face of reality.

Existential analysis meets clients at the profoundly human level. Therapy necessarily places its initial focus on individuals as they present themselves sitting before the therapist, but the therapeutic approach, based on dialogue between client and therapist, presumes encounter and negates the critique that the therapist is neutral or an objective by-stander. On the contrary, the therapist encounters another human being within this dialogue, and this opens the door to analyzing the ethical stand occurring between therapist and client, a stand that reflects the ethical posture embedded in all human encounter. The therapist confronts the client's experiences, feelings, and thoughts. Each of the client's highly individualized statements is a simultaneous expression of familial, social, ethical, and religious meanings, values, and aspirations. Dialogue within therapy reveals the complex relationship between inner and outer reality. Therapists encounter all of this within the dialogues they have with their clients. The therapist, too, is subsequently challenged, moved, and changed by the encounter.

The Four Fundamental Existential Motivations

The theory of existential analysis is structured around what are called the four fundamental existential motivations. Using the first person, let me illustrate. My motivations as an individual are activated by the continuous engagement and dialogue I have with the world around me. I am essentially called, confronted, and provoked by life. I, in turn, must respond to this calling and be active with my whole being. Human existence, from an existential analytic perspective, is fueled by these four basic and fundamental motivations, and they make up the structure of existence within the theoretical model of existential analysis. Each of the four motivations, in turn, corresponds to (or dialogues with) a respective existential reality or pillar. The first fundamental motivation corresponds to the world, the second to life, the third to self, and the fourth to the future. Each motivation involves an encounter and confrontation with a fundamental question of existence. Because we are essentially "dialogical," our being confronted or questioned by the world, by life, and by other human beings demands our active response and participation. In turn, the concrete expressions that mark our unique responses and how we choose to participate in the world stem from our individual perceptions and experiences of these fundamental questions.

The first fundamental existential motivation corresponds to my very existence. "I exist." "I am here." "I am in this world." As Längle states, the very fact that I, as a human being, am conscious of this fundamental question of existence places an existential question before me, that being "Can I be?" or "How do I exist?" The monumental scope of such questions is tempered by our personal experiences of the following: Do I experience *protection, space, and support?* Do I feel protected and accepted? Do I feel at home somewhere? Where do I find support in my life? The highly subjective experiences we have that our very existence is protected and supported and that our existence is reliably "held" leads to further experiences of trust and faith in the world and confidence in ourselves. We can see that these experiences encompass a vast range, from parental, familial, societal, or institutional to experiences of divine support and protection. Whether or not support and protection is, in fact, experienced depends on the kind of support and protection a family, culture, or society either deems appropriate or is capable of providing. However, lacking an experiential base of protection and support, Längle states that we may experience insecurity, fear, and restlessness.

Dialogue with the world incorporates both my experience and my subsequent participation and action in the world. In this first category, my active participation and dialogue with the world necessitates my acceptance and endurance of the conditions of life and not an attempt to flee from them. It requires that I realistically acknowledge and accept the realities and facts into which I am embedded. Längle states,

> To accept means to be ready to occupy the space that I am in, to rely on the support given and to trust the protection bestowed on me; in short "to be here" and not to flee. To endure requires the fortitude to accept whatever may be difficult, menacing or unalterable and to tolerate what cannot be changed. Life imposes certain conditions on me; the world has its laws to which I must adapt. This idea is expressed in the word "subject" in the sense of "not independent," of being subject to. On the other hand these same conditions of the world are reliable, solid and steady despite the boundaries they impose. I can allow them to be and accept them if I can be at the same time. To accept means letting the other be, whether a person, a thing or a situation. It means that I can be and the other can be equally because there is still enough space for me and the circumstances do not threaten my being here.[17]

The second fundamental existential motivation extends from the first. Once we have our space in the world, we fill it with life. We want our existence to have value since it is more than mere fact. This places a fundamental existential question of life before me. "I am alive." "Do I like this?" "Is it good to be here?" "Do I truly live?" The answers to these questions are experienced and embodied within our dialogue with the world, specifically through *relationship, time, and closeness* with others. Our experiences of relationship and closeness, for example, lead to a harmonious feeling within ourselves and that, in turn, extends outward toward the world generally. If I am valued and experience this from others, I value myself and then value others. If I have the experience that what I do in life is recognized by others, validated, and affirmed, then I have a sense of my place in the world and that my existence is of value. Simultaneously, that experience of outer recognition and value is experienced internally as self-value and projects outward again as I, in turn, value others I encounter. Within the fundamental existential motivations we see a continuous balance between individual experience and the reality of interdependence with the world around us.

A life lacking in experiences of relationship, time, and closeness can lead to feelings of longing, depression, and a deliberate distancing of ourselves from others. As with the first fundamental motivation, my obligation as an individual capable of decision is to access my freedom and responsibility and be actively engaged in my development. Therefore, my

---

[17] Längle, "Search for Meaning in Life," 32.

active participation is to engage in life and allow myself to be both close to others and touched by others. Längle states, "I must seize life by engaging with life. When I turn to other people...I turn towards life. When I move towards something or someone, allow myself to get close, allow myself to be touched, I experience life as vibrant."[18]

The third fundamental existential motivation corresponds to my experiences and feelings of singularity and uniqueness in the midst of, and never divorced from, my being related to the people and the world around me. These experiences and awareness place the following existential questions of being before me. "I am myself; do I feel free to be myself?" "Do I have the right to be who I am and behave as I do?" The ethical demand on me raises still further questions: "Who am I?" "Who am I capable of becoming?" "Who should I become?" Answering these questions requires dialogue with the world in simultaneous conjunction with our subjective experiences of *attention, justice, and appreciation.* Experiencing these leads to self-esteem, self-respect, and living authentically. Without these, we may experience solitude and shame.

Again, my active participation or responsibility is to say "yes" to myself, to affirm my being. My encounter and dialogue with others in addition to my care and appreciation of others creates an equal appreciation of myself. Allowing myself to encounter another person in his or her uniqueness, being capable of delineating my own uniqueness, and accessing my ability to stand on my own lends itself to the experience of personal affirmation, the "yes." This particular motivation is useful in discussing issues of ethics and identity, self and other, individuality and community.

The question "Who am I?" relates to the discovery of self within dialogue, the discovery of self in the midst of this world. The questions "Who am I capable of becoming?" and "Who should I become?" are those of an individual who is firmly embedded in the circumstances, connections, conditions, contexts, and "facts" of his or her life. Answers to these questions necessitate not only an awareness of subjective feeling and experience, they benefit in depth and substance from dialogue with the concrete social and cultural structures and institutions as well as the more ambiguous arena of culturally shaped and perpetuated ethics, meanings, and values.

---

[18] Ibid., 33.

These dialogues raise creative, ethical, and illuminating questions about the extent to which internal psychological development and fulfillment are inextricably linked to the external world. They have the potential to reveal the extent to which my development and psychological well-being are linked to culturally sanctioned ideologies of how we should and ought to behave and what the normal parameters of human behavior and conduct are. My active participation at this level requires my reflection and response: What am I confronted with or questioned by, and how do I respond? My participation requires my acknowledgment that I am a unique individual, discernible yet shaped by larger cultural contexts and values, be they familial, cultural, religious, economic, or political.

The fourth fundamental existential motivation corresponds to the meaning and purpose of my existence. It is not enough to merely "find ourselves" or value self-actualization as our primary goal (as popular psychological parlance often states). Viktor Frankl frequently commented that our Western cultural preoccupation with self-actualization should not, in fact, be a goal in and of itself. We do not live merely for ourselves. We live for something or someone. Although we are aware of and experience our singularity and uniqueness, we also orient our existence beyond ourselves toward others. Our development as human beings is not static; it has movement and direction and is oriented outward with aim and purpose. Although many psychological theories highlight self-discovery and self-actualization as the aim and goal of successful therapy, both Frankl and particularly Längle see our human development and fulfillment in terms of relational possibility, meaning, and value. As such, to experience our lives as fulfilling and meaningful requires us to transcend our individuality. This means reaching outward in dialogue and being engaged and active in the world around us. At this level, we are confronted with a fundamental question about the meaning of our existence. "I am here—for what purpose?" The factual reality of my existence is placed in immediate context, and possible answers to this question come through my experiences within *a field of activity, a structural context, and a value to be realized in the future.* This puts me once again in dialogue with the contexts, activities, shared values, and meanings that simultaneously evoke my individual responsibility, my freedom, my creative possibilities, and my decisions. Similar to Frankl's idea of the actualization of creative, experiential, and attitudinal values, Längle contends that we need specific activities to be engaged in and that we need to contribute to the world. We need structure in our lives and contexts in which to experience the value of contribution and connection. As we saw in William Doherty's illustration about the experiences of the psychological reductionism endured by many of his clients when they expressed their desires to be socially and ethically engaged, existential analysis acknowledges the enormous value in our actively engaging in the development and potential changes to the world around us.

Since existence from an existential perspective is seen as a process of becoming that points toward the future, the fulfillment and meaning we experience through the goals we strive for evoke further feelings of hope, trust, and faith in the future. These experiences make us capable of dedication and action. Our committed response to the world provides meaning and a profound sense of fulfillment. Without these experiences, feelings of emptiness, frustration, despair, and addiction often arise.

With each motivation, we have an individual responsibility, literally doing our part in actualizing meaning and fulfillment in our lives. This is done through our active participation in the world and requires a phenomenological attitude. Frankl often stated that life asks us questions to which we have an ethical responsibility to respond. The dialogical nature of existential analysis follows a very similar line of thought. Every situation in life places a demand or question before me. How I respond represents the existential access to meaning in life. Do I, for example, respond with an attitude of openness toward others and the world? What can I do, what am I capable of in this situation? What should I do in this moment? Is what I am doing a good thing (What kind of choice have I made?), is it right for others, for me, for the future, for the environment? This fourth motivation corresponds to issues of personal responsibility and possibility. If one were to analyze each of these questions, we would find that an attitude of openness requires a level of trust and faith. In other words, if human existence is dialogical and I have experienced protection, support, relationships, and appreciation and have actively responded by participating in the world, I am more likely to have an attitude of trust and openness toward the world. This motivates me to invest once again in the dialogical process and exercise my moral imperative: to become, as Tillich would have it, a person within a community of persons.

Paul Tillich and Alfried Längle's Theory of Existential Analysis: A Dialogue

Once again, I would like to offer a brief illustration that links the voices from the past with contemporary theory. In this case, I would like to bring Tillich's ideas and the theory of existential analysis together in dialogue.

By drawing psychological and theological issues together, we have seen a number of recurrent themes: the meaning of health and well-being, the constituents of a meaningful and productive existence, the meaning of care and relationship, and the ethical subtexts of each of these at both the individual and cultural level. What follows is a brief illustration of the links that can be made between Tillich's experiential description of sin as separation and estrangement and Längle's emphasis on human potential. Further, Tillich's proposed means of overcoming sin through acceptance and reconciliation corresponds to the emphasis on hope, possibility, affirmation, and dialogue that characterizes psychological health in the theory of existential analysis.

As we have continually seen throughout this book, the discipline of psychology has been, and continues to be, somewhat reticent about addressing issues of personal responsibility, meaning, values, and belief. All of these are seen to be outside the parameters of what psychology and therapy do, yet each of these involves experiential and behavioral expressions replete with ethical and moral subtexts that psychology often prefers to ignore. Längle's theory of existential analysis, however, is expanding psychology's mandate greatly by confronting both the reality and ambiguity of individual and cultural expression and experience. Theories such as existential analysis allow for fruitful interaction with Tillich's theological thought and illustrate the profound experiential insight he continues to offer for the expansion of psychological theory. Approaches such as the one I am suggesting not only keep Tillich's thought relevant, they challenge psychology to confront and possibly expand its own implicit visions, beliefs, constructions, and idealizations of both the healthy individual and the healthy society.

Acutely aware of psychology's discomfort with ethical issues, Tillich challenged his psychological colleagues within the New York Psychology

Group[19] to acknowledge that ethics were indeed entrenched within psychological visions of who we are and of what we are capable. Further, in *Systematic Theology*, Tillich listed the discipline of psychology, among others, as capable of explaining estrangement in deterministic terms, but, he noted, "None of these explanations accounts for the feeling of personal responsibility that man has for his acts of sin and separation."[20] While Tillich felt that existential analyses (and I presume he meant philosophical analyses) were helpful in describing the human predicament, he also felt it was necessary to develop a realistic doctrine of humankind that would address and balance both the ethical (actualizing our human potential for dialogue and love) and what he called the tragic elements of human life. His views resonate several decades later with contemporary discussions about the possible, and necessary, dialogue between science and religion. Ian Barbour's contemporary debate in this particular arena, for example, reminds us that psychological theory is constrained by strict ideologies of scientific and theoretical rationality. To borrow a very apt critique from Barbour, theories about psychological growth and development arise from "acts of creative imagination."[21] At the same time, the area of personal meaning cannot be relegated strictly to the religious domain. Psychology, indeed therapy itself, deals with profound experiential expressions of personal meaning. Therapy engages more often than not in acts of creative imagination and dialogue rather than recognizable categories of pathology.

Stepping forward from the disciplinary limitations Tillich aptly described, his concept of sin can be juxtaposed with Längle's theory of existential analysis. Tillich's immense interest in psychology and his own profoundly astute observations on human nature and human experience have a great affinity with existential analysis. Existential analysis's acknowledgement of the ambiguity and near impossibility of fully capturing what it is to be human nevertheless confronts and incorporates these multiple paradoxes into its theoretical framework, allowing hope,

---

[19] The New York Psychology Group of the National Council on Religion and Higher Education, 1941–1945, hereafter cited as NYPG. From the collection of Prof. Allison Stokes of Ithaca College, New York.

[20] Paul Tillich, *Systematic Theology*, vol. 2 (Chicago: University of Chicago Press, 1967) 56–57.

[21] Ian G. Barbour, *When Science Meets Religion* (New York: HarperCollins, 2000) 25–26.

possibility, and acceptance into its vision of health and healing. Among the ambiguities are the finiteness of our biological make-up along with the infinite potential and possibility we possess throughout our lives, our individual freedom to actualize and express our potential and creativity along with our equal responsibility to "other," our capacity to experience both joy and tragedy, and our ability to decide and take a stand despite the anxiety such choices may produce. Certainly a theory open to these realities, capabilities, and possibilities moves psychology toward a far more expansive interdisciplinary approach, one that includes the religious and ethical expressions of being human.

Tillich's definition of sin emphasizes the personal and individual experience of being separated and estranged. For Tillich, this included our experiences of being separated from ourselves, from each other or the world around us, and from God. While human existence is characterized as being ambiguously both separated from yet united with the ground of being, this fundamental characteristic of existence implies that sin is a universal condition. Yet Tillich's description of sin as a personal decision at the experiential level of turning away "from that to which one belongs"[22]—the separating of ourselves from ourselves, from others, and from God—evokes psychological expressions of individual responsibility, choice, and freedom.

The choice and subsequent act of separation imply some degree of personal responsibility in one's own estrangement. As human beings, we are free to turn away psychologically, experientially, and spiritually from our potential. We are free to turn away from the depth and meaning of our lives, free to turn away from our very humanity. We are free to turn away through decisive acts of physical and psychological isolation and separation, such as hatred, anger, cynicism, prejudice, destructive acts toward ourselves and others, along with attitudes we covet that break the possibility for dialogue or union. Of course, there are instances of neurological and biological pathology that can cause such actions. But much of counseling and therapy does not occur within frameworks of pathology. Rather, it engages in individual experiential levels of meaninglessness, despair, emptiness, and relational conflict. Each of these is a psychological break or

[22] Tillich, *Systematic Theology*, vol. 2, 46.

schism in dialogue and interconnectedness. In Tillichian terms, they are the manifestations of estrangement and separation.

Our estrangement and separation from ourselves, from others, from our aim and purpose in life, from the mystery, depth, and greatness of our existence is felt through these experiences of meaninglessness, emptiness, cynicism, and distance. At the profoundly personal level, our inability to probe what Tillich described as the deeper levels of reality leads us toward separation and estrangement as opposed to acceptance and reconciliation through both self-affirmation and love of others. This is experienced through an inability to ask questions about the world and ourselves and an inability to accept the ambiguity and precariousness of human life through experiences both meaningless and meaningful. Tillich writes, "No one is willing to acknowledge in concrete terms his finitude, his weakness and his errors, his ignorance and his insecurity, his loneliness and his anxiety."[23]

Tillich described our moral imperative as becoming a person within a community of persons. "A moral act," he wrote, "is not an act in which some divine or human law is obeyed but an act in which life integrates itself in the dimension of the spirit, and this means as personality within a com-munity."[24] The development of selfhood was for Tillich inextricably linked and bound to an ethical relationship with others and the world around us. He emphasized the interdependence of a centered self and a structured universe. Again, Tillich's astute understanding of the subject/object split within many psychological theories is reoriented in his vision of positive human development as situated in the midst and within the inevitable complexity of interrelationship.

In a similar vein, existential analysis describes human existence as fundamentally dialogical. Human life is the interdependence of self and other. Psychological growth, development, health, and well-being are predi-cated on our freedom, responsibility, and capacity to actualize and fulfill our human potential. That potential is to maintain, balance, and express the essence of our humanity. This includes our dialogical nature, the coordination of intrapersonal and interpersonal dialogue and the striving for a deeper understanding of our experiences and actions. Our individual po-tential mirrors our human potential. As Längle has stated,

---

[23] Ibid., 51.

[24] Tillich, *Systematic Theology*, vol. 3, 38.

"In the midst of this world, I discover myself unmistakably." The development of selfhood, indeed, the ability to develop and express our individual human potential, is predicated on an ongoing dialogue, engagement, and participation with the world. Therapy from such an existential analytic perspective focuses on how we encounter the world; how we integrate the world around us; how we contribute to the world; how we respond, accept, or challenge the facts of our existence; how we construct meaning; and, finally, how we live creatively. All of these are seen within the contexts of both subjective and shared experience. Psychological growth, health, and development, as we saw earlier, are contingent upon our engagement and response to the world, requiring us to think, feel, react, and participate both subjectively and beyond our subjectivity by transcending creatively through faith, hope, love, possibility, decision, and action.

Contained within the dialogical emphasis of existential analysis is the idea that individual well-being, including psychological health and development, is linked to our human capacity for responsibility and the ability to weigh ethically, through decision and choice, what binds us together as human beings and how we must treat one another. Tillich and Längle would similarly argue that actualizing deeper and more authentic layers of human potential rests within, and never apart from, dialogue with ourselves, with others, and the world around us.

As we have seen, human existence from an existential analytic perspective is marked by what Längle terms the four cornerstones of existence: the world, life, self, and the future. Briefly, the world embraces facts, potentials, and supporting structures; life corresponds to our network of feelings and relationships; self means existing as an autonomous individual who is unique and dignified; and the future corresponds to our human ability to decide or choose a course of action, construct meaningful ways of living and behaving, seeing the future as possibility, and activating our capacity for value and hope. The process of becoming and authentic psychological growth, development, and health necessitates a continuous dialogue with each of these four cornerstones. It requires an acknowledgement that our individuality both influences and is influenced by the world around us. Längle adds four fundamental existential motivations, which correspond, as a dialogical partner, with the four cornerstones of existence. To review, the first existential motivation corresponds to the world and evokes the fundamental existential question: "I exist, I am in the world, can I be?" Dialogue emerges between an individual's experience of protection, space, and support from the world and that individual's active response of accepting and enduring the conditions the world presents. The second fundamental motivation corresponds to life and evokes the fundamental question "I am alive, do I truly live?" Experiencing relationship and closeness with others is balanced by an individual's active engagement with life by allowing him- or herself to be close to others and touched by others. The third fundamental motivation corresponds to selfhood. Our capacity to be aware of our singularity and uniqueness in spite of our being related to others places before us the following fundamental question of being: "I am myself, do I have the right to be who I am and behave as I do?" Experiencing attention, justice, and appreciation activates an individual response, one that dignifies our uniqueness, allows us to affirm our singularity, yet also enables us to care for others. Finally, the fourth fundamental motivation corresponds to the future. The fundamental question addressing the meaning of our existence is placed before us: "I am here, for what purpose?" Experiencing a field of activity, a structural context, and a value to be realized in the future activates our human capacity for dedication and action, meaning and fulfillment. An individual's active dialogue and response to this fundamental question is centered on an attitude of openness, possibility, and responsibility toward the world. "What does this moment, this situation expect from me?" "Is what I am doing a good thing; is it right for others, for me, for the future, for the environment?"

Therapy in such a context requires that the therapist engage in a dialogue with the patient; indeed, it is the therapist's own involved attitude of hope, possibility, and affirmation that distinguishes existential analysis. The therapeutic emphasis on hope and possibility, an emphasis that incorporates an ethic of care, acceptance, and responsibility, reveals the transcendent nature of this kind of therapeutic approach. Psychological health is situated simultaneously within our singular uniqueness and our capacity to respond to and be engaged with life. A therapist who conveys an ethic of care, concern, possibility, and hope extends this to the patient. Such an approach echoes Tillich's idea of the moral imperative. To become a person within a community of persons is equivalent to the therapeutic process of existential analysis that situates psychological health and healing within dialogical encounter (specifically, the activation of the four fundamental motivations) and never within isolated subjectivity. Tillich saw the danger implied in what he called the "empty shell of subjectivity."[25] He felt the emphasis on isolated subjectivity, so prevalent in psychology of separating the individual from participation, as the mark of estrangement. Overcoming this in order to maintain what he considered the unity of being required the acknowledgment of the mutual relationship between individualization and participation. This corresponds with Längle's opinion, state earlier, that the essence of our human and individual spirit is "a spirit that is looking out for participation, dialogue, creativity and possibility."[26]

From an existential perspective, psychological health is based in part on the idea that human life is an ongoing process of development, an ongoing process toward selfhood. Inextricably linked with dialogue and the implications of ethical confrontation and relations with others, the goal of psychological health is both an increasing knowledge of ourselves and the ability to reach beyond ourselves and know others. This includes our ability to be open, receptive, and loving toward others and ourselves. It requires that we activate our human capacities for responsibility, freedom, and decision.

Tillich's description of sin as separation, estrangement, and a turning away from our human potential at the experiential level has valuable links with existential analysis and its perspective on psychological health and development. As stated, psychological illness and distress is the result of a breakdown or schism in dialogue and relation, both within and without. This breakdown prohibits our individual and collective potential as human beings to live our lives with greater depth, meaning, and responsibility. This includes our ability to activate our human potential for love, care, and community. The overcoming of separation and estrangement for Tillich is at one level a personal choice of action through love and faith, a purposeful striving and turning toward ourselves and others in reunion. Love, Tillich described, was "life itself in its actual unity."[27] Where love embodied itself, life was possible. Where love embodied itself, "life is maintained and

---

[25] Tillich, *Systematic Theology*, vol. 2, 65.

[26] Längle, "Search for Meaning in Life," 29.

[27] Paul Tillich, *The Protestant Era* (Chicago: The University of Chicago Press, 1957) 160.

saved."[28] Love, Tillich described, was the affirmation of self and other, and love characterized the genuine relatedness and acceptance embodied in the I/Thou encounter. Always psychologically astute, Tillich stressed the importance of love (both the receiving and giving of love) in becoming a person, important in maintaining psychological health and development. In an interview with humanistic psychologist Carl Rogers, Tillich referred poetically to "listening love"[29] to describe the encounter between therapist and client in conveying genuine dialogue, relatedness, care, compassion, and hope.

These acts of freedom and responsibility toward reconciliation are similar to Längle's notions of psychological health and positive, purposeful development. Psychological health is the outcome of directed, intentional action and interrelationship. Health is both the turning toward ourselves in self-affirmation and self-acceptance and the turning toward others with openness, love, and respect. Dialogue enables us to know ourselves with greater depth. It challenges us to assess realistically our capabilities and our failings. It situates our development as human beings beyond mere subjectivity. And it requires us to be receptive to others, allowing ourselves to be touched by others and revealing our capacity to care for others. Dialogue and engagement require us to use our human freedom for choice and decision by assessing what life asks of us and to be engaged with life at a moral and ethical level.

While many psychological theories tend to neglect these more philosophical demands, they are paramount to the health and well-being of individuals and how "healthy" individuals engage with the world around them. The attitude persists within many psychological circles that such matters are not the domain or responsibility of therapists and theorists. Yet Tillich and Längle both see the interrelationship between the individual and community as vital to health and development. During the four years Tillich spent with the New York Psychology Group, several overriding questions influenced the discussions. What made a human being truly human? Could we identify humane behavior? Were these behaviors universal? How could theology and psychology promote humane action? Should psychology even be engaged in what amounted to an ethical

[28] Ibid.

[29] *Carl Rogers: Dialogues*, eds. Howard Kirschenbaum and Valerie Land Henderson (Boston: Houghton Mifflin Company, 1969): 78.

directive? Members of the group strongly believed that neither psychology nor theology alone could fully capture the constituents of human nature. They collectively agreed that these questions might never be answered but that they must remain active. In fact, members of the NYPG clearly felt that a position of hope and possibility pushed intellectual debate further. Decades later, Alfried Längle would similarly argue that positioning psychological theory within the confines of pathology limits the discipline's ability to help and heal. Indeed, by limiting psychology's scope, theoreticians and practitioners are denied any possibility of seeing psychological health as the activation and maintenance of positive, creative, and loving human potential.

Engaging the thought of theologian Paul Tillich with contemporary existential psychological theory offers an illustration of how we can expand our vision of human experience and potential, perhaps offering an avenue for more realistic assessments of human nature.

Conclusion

The fundamental existential questions we have explored in Längle's theory of existential analysis are not singularly psychological questions. They are open-ended and resound with multiple meanings and ethical interpretations of what human existence is and what we wish to strive for and accomplish as human beings. These questions, reflected in therapy by clients who are attempting to understand and fully grasp the meaning and value of their existence, point to how open psychological health and well-being are to interpretation. Längle's statement in the title of this final chapter assumes the fluidity of concepts such as "world" and "I." From an existential perspective, the discovery of who I am is an ongoing process open to change. From this perspective, a concept of self does not assume it is either fixed or stable. What constitutes self is sometimes identifiable, sometimes elusive. A unique and distinguishable "I" simultaneously depends on and draws meaning from the world.

We saw illustrations in the previous chapter of the contemporary critique that an emphasis on self-actualization and self-fulfillment, so prevalent in our "therapeutic" age, gives way to a general belief that there is a "stable innate self" that has the right to prioritize self-expression over and above the rights of community. Existential analysis, as we have seen, would not presume a separate and identifiable self. Rather, the self is discovered continuously within relationship. Therefore, fundamental existential questions such as "Who am I?" engage psychotherapy in a deeper dialogue of personal and collective values, ethics, and beliefs. The meaning of my unique existence rests within the dialogues I have with the wider culture of which I am part, and this, existential analysis suggests, raises the possibility of analyzing and contributing to the ethical and moral connections between individual and cultural development. The dialogue between the individual and the social/cultural raises the issue of an individual's moral and ethical response as a human being. It harkens back to the historical voices we have explored, and, in this chapter, to Jaspers's comment about the potential that resides in each individual spark. Valuing the individual and community as interrelated puts more trust and faith in individuals and the ethical power they may exercise toward the world.

Existential analysis has (like any psychological theory, as Frankl pointed out, but as few theories actually acknowledge) a philosophy of human nature at its core. Existential analysis situates human nature within a "multidimensional unity," to borrow a phrase from Tillich. Therapy, from this philosophical perspective, reflects this multidimensionality. The dialogues that take place within therapy are both personal and collective expressions of possibility against shifting backdrops of reality. These dialogues expose what it is to be human, what it is to experience and express faith, and what is both constructed and experienced as meaningful. These dialogues express ethical statements as well as cultural norms and expectations. Therapeutic dialogues within existential analysis expose a client's experiences of relationship, support, community, isolation, and despair. The experiences clients have of their relationships to and with the outside world extend to highly personal experiences they have of themselves. Existential analysis encourages the expression of these experiences through dialogue in therapy and, by doing so, keeps fundamental questions about our existence alive.

7

Concluding Remarks

> Therapy has a moral purpose because it rests on the assumption that internal harmony and a capacity for personal growth and responsibility are better than emotional conflict, anxiety and self-enslavement. In serving this purpose it is fostering a humanitarian end which is analogous to religious salvation.[1]

The historical illustrations we have examined represent substantial dialogues between theology and psychology that ultimately remind us of many enduring themes, including the ambiguous and mysterious character of human life and whether we can accept this ambiguity and work with it theoretically. Can we be satisfied with creative questioning and dialogue?

The profound dialogue that took place in the mid-twentieth century between theologians and psychologists raised issues that touched both individual and cultural development. The New York Psychology Group,[2] Viktor Frankl, and the Harvard Project on Religion and Mental Health bridged many gaps between two powerful cultural discourses, psychology and theology, through their commitment to positive, ethically grounded human potential. These groups and individuals made substantial contributions to some of the following issues: the aim and purpose of psychology within Western culture; the moral and ethical foundations of psychological theory; and the conceptualizations of humankind implicit in every psychological theory, including the implications these same concepts had when they were (and are) applied to assumptions about individual and cultural development and fulfillment.

---

[1] David E. Roberts, *Psychotherapy and a Christian View of Man* (New York: Charles Scribner's Sons, 1950) 40.

[2] The New York Psychology Group of the National Council on Religion and Higher Education, 1941–1945, hereafter cited as NYPG. From the collection of Prof. Allison Stokes of Ithaca College, New York.

As we saw, psychology was not singled out. Theology, too, came under scrutiny. The perception that traditional theology was increasingly irrelevant to the twentieth century fueled a renewed desire to discuss and analyze both religion's place within Western culture and the role of the minister in relation to his parishioners. Joining together in dialogue, certain individuals from these two powerful domains believed that despite the respective boundaries of their fields, they had one important thing in common: maintaining the value and dignity of human life.

The dialogues between psychology and theology explored in this book also offer a rich perspective and context from which to assess many contemporary voices in the field of psychology. As we saw in the two final chapters, critical psychology and existential analysis, although offering very different approaches and perspectives to psychological study and the therapeutic encounter, have much to gain from connections with the past. In the case of existential analysis, it has direct roots in a theory and therapy from the past, that being Viktor Frankl's Logotherapy. Yet it is also an example of a contemporary psychotherapy that embodies the rich ethical, compassionate, and humane tone—including dialogue itself—of the dialogues of the past between theologians and psychologists. As for critical psychology, there is an ironic contrast between its serious and pointed critique of psychology and its own lack of awareness of historical, religious, and ethical context. I hope a continued examination of the dialogues from the past, particularly interdisciplinary ones, will contribute to our reflection on similar and enduring questions, all of which are based on an enduring aspiration: to discover what it means to be human. Always in the background of these enduring questions is the possibility of change and of discovering greater depths of human potential; the possibility, as David E. Roberts suggests, of salvation.

The view that human existence is essentially relational is not new and was not discovered by postmodern theory but, in fact, is well grounded in history. This book has attempted to expose the relationship, as opposed to the contrast, between individual and cultural expressions of freedom, responsibility, care, and justice. Individually and collectively, we have a choice, indeed an obligation, as human beings to progress psychologically and spiritually in ways that are positive and constructive for humankind as a whole. "What seldom occurs to us," Hans Hofmann once wrote, "is that the fault may not lie in either the people or the world but in their relation to each other."[3]

Is it possible to maintain a relationship between the dignity of the individual and our collective participation in the public good? Is this within the realm and scope of psychology? If not, should psychology expand its mandate to include dialogues that address this relationship? Isaac Prilleltensky has suggested that psychology must find a balance between the individual and the collective. Finding this balance is a difficult but necessary task and requires psychology to open itself to collaborations with which it has historically been uncomfortable, including those associated with religion, philosophy, and ethics. The motivation to continue the dialogue and the questioning comes, in part, from a belief in the human potential for change. The British moral philosopher Mary Midgley sees these as impossibly large yet worthy avenues of inquiry. They do, in fact, produce more questions and leave us in even more ambiguous waters. As Midgley states,

> Human beings are distinctive in being enormously more aware than other creatures both of their individuality and of the factors, both inside and outside them, that compromise it. They can think and talk and argue about these things, so can they share much of their experience and help each other with these problems. They can be aware of forces that are prolonging or changing their ways of life and they can, if they wish, direct their efforts to supporting or resisting them. Our unity as individuals is not something given. It is a continuing, lifelong project, an effort constantly undertaken in the face of disintegrating forces.[4]

Not only is Midgley correct, but these questions reflect the ongoing struggle to bring issues and concerns about individual and community well-being together as obvious partners in dialogue instead of seeing them as perpetually in opposition.

---

[3] Hans Hofmann, *Discovering Freedom* (Boston: Beacon Press, 1969) 13.

[4] Mary Midgley, *The Ethical Primate: Humans, Freedom and Morality* (London: Routledge, 1996) 23.

Bibliography

Academy of Religion and Mental Health. *Religion, Culture and Mental Health: Proceedings of the Third Academy Symposium, 1959.* New York: New York University Press, 1961.

———. *Religion in the Developing Personality: Proceedings of the Second Academy Symposium, 1958.* New York: New York University Press, 1960.

———. *Religion, Science and Mental Health: Proceedings of the First Academy Symposium on Inter-discipline Responsibility for Mental Health, 1957.* New York: New York University Press, 1959.

Appel, Kenneth E. "The Present Challenge of Psychiatry." *American Journal of Psychiatry* 111 (1968).

Aspects in Contexts: Studies in the History of Psychology of Religion. Edited by Jacob A. Belzen. Amsterdam, Netherlands: Editions Rodopi BV, 2000.

Barbour, Ian G. *When Science Meets Religion: Enemies, Strangers or Partners?* New York: HarperCollins, 2000.

Browning, Don S. "Analogy, Symbol, and Pastoral Theology in Tillich's Thought." *Pastoral Psychology* 19/181 (February 1968).

———. *A Fundamental Practical Theology: Descriptive and Strategic Proposals.* Minneapolis MN: Fortress Press, 1996.

———. *Generative Man: Psychoanalytic Perspectives.* Philadelphia: Westminster Press, 1973.

———. *The Moral Context of Pastoral Care.* Philadelphia: Westminster Press, 1976.

———. *Religious Ethics and Pastoral Care.* Philadelphia: Fortress Press, 1983.

Browning, Don S. and Terry D. Cooper. *Religious Thought and Modern Psychologies.* Minneapolis: Fortress Press, 2004.

Buber, Martin. *I and Thou.* New York: Charles Scribner's Sons, 1970.

Bugental, James F. T. *Psychotherapy and Process: The Fundamentals of an Existential-Humanistic Psychotherapy.* London: Sage Publications, 1978.

Bulman, Raymond F. and Frederick J. Parrella. *A Blueprint for Humanity: Paul Tillich's Theology of Culture.* Lewisburg PA: Bucknell University Press, 1981.

———. *Religion in the New Millennium: Theology in the Spirit of Paul Tillich.* Macon GA: Mercer University Press, 2001.

Burr, Vivien. *The Person in Social Psychology.* New York: Taylor & Francis, 2002.

Cali, Grace. *Paul Tillich First-Hand: A Memoir of the Harvard Years.* Chicago: Exploration Press, 1966.

Carl Rogers: Dialogues. Edited by Howard Kirschenbaum and Valerie Land Henderson. Boston: Houghton Mifflin, 1989.

Carrington, W. L. *Psychology, Religion, and Human Need: A Guide for Ministers, Physicians, Teachers, and Social Workers.* Great Neck NY: Channel Press, 1957.

Challenging Subjects: Critical Psychology for a New Millennium. Edited by Valerie Walkerdine. Hampshire and New York: Palgrave, 2002.

Changing the Subject: Psychology, Social Regulation and Subjectivity. Edited by Julian Henriques, Wendy Hollway, Cathy Urwin, Couze Venn, and Valerie Walkerdine. London and New York: Routledge, 1998.

Christianity and the Existentialists. Edited by Carl Michalson. Charles Scribner's Sons, 1956.

Cohn, Hans W. *Existential Thought and Therapeutic Practice: An Introduction to Existential Psychotherapy.* London: Sage Publications, 1997.

Cooper, Terry D. *Paul Tillich and Psychology: Historic and Contemporary Explorations in Theology, Psychotherapy, and Ethics.* Macon GA: Mercer University Press, 2006.

———. *Sin, Pride and Self-Acceptance: The Problem of Identity in Theology and Psychology.* Downer's Grove IL: InterVarsity Press, 2003.

Cornett, Carlton. *The Soul of Psychotherapy: Recapturing the Spiritual Dimension in the Therapeutic Encounter.* New York: The Free Press, 1998.

Cottingham, John. *The Spiritual Dimension: Religion, Philosophy and Human Value.* Cambridge: Cambridge University Press, 2005.

Critical Psychology: An Introduction. Edited by Dennis Fox and Isaac Prilleltensky. London: Sage Publications, 1997.

Cushman, Philip. *Constructing the Self, Constructing America: A Cultural History of Psychotherapy.* New York: Da Capo Press, 1995.

Danziger, Kurt. *Constructing the Subject: Historical Origins of Psychological Research.* Cambridge: Cambridge University Press, 1990.

"A Decade of Postmodern Psychology." In *Postmodern Psychologies, Societal Practice, and Political Life.* Edited by Lois Holzman and John Morss. New York: Routledge, 2000.

The Dialogue Between Theology and Psychology. Voume 3. Edited by Peter Homans. Chicago: University of Chicago Press, 1968.

Doherty, William J. *Soul Searching: Why Psychology Must Promote Moral Responsibility.* New York: Basic Books, 1995.

Dueck, Alvin C. *Between Jerusalem and Athens: Ethical Perspectives on Culture, Religion and Psychotherapy.* Grand Rapids MI: Baker Books, 1995.

Dueck, Alvin C. and Kevin Reimer. "Religious Discourse in Psychotherapy." *International Journal of Existential Psychology and Psychotherapy* 1/1 (July 2004): 3–15.

Embodies Theories. Edited by Ernesto Spinelli and Sue Marshall. London and New York: Continuum, 2001.

Emmons, Robert A. *The Psychology of Ultimate Concerns: Motivation and Spirituality in Personality.* New York: Guilford Press, 1999.

Fontana, David. *Psychology, Religion, and Spirituality.* Victoria, Australia: Blackwell, 2003.

Frankl, Viktor E. *The Doctor and the Soul.* New York: Vintage Books, 1986.

———. *Dr. Viktor E. Frankl's Salute to RIUE's 20th Anniversary.* Viktor E. Frankl Collection, GTU 98-5-012, Graduate Theological Union Archives, Flora Lawson Hewitt Library, Graduate Theological Union, Berkeley CA. Audiotape. 28 August 1966.

———. *Existential Dynamics and Neurotic Escapism.* Viktor E. Frankl Collection, GTU 98-5-012, Graduate Theological Union Archives, Flora Lawson Hewitt Library, Graduate Theological Union, Berkeley CA. Audiotape. Presented to the Academy of Religion and Health, 17 May 1962.

———. *Man's Search for Meaning.* New York: Washington Square Press, 1985.

———. *Man's Search for Ultimate Meaning.* New York: Plenum Press, 1997.

———. *Psychotherapy and Existentialism.* New York: Simon and Schuster, 1967.

———. *The Unconscious God.* New York: Washington Square Press, 1985.

———. *The Unheard Cry for Meaning.* New York: Washington Square Press, 1985.

———. *U.S. Nation Tour: Harvard: 20–27 September 1957.* Viktor E. Frankl Collection, GTU 98-5-012, Graduate Theological Union Archives, Flora Lawson Hewitt Library, Graduate Theological Union, Berkeley CA. Master lecture manuscript.

———. *U.S. Nation Tour: Harvard: September 20–27, 1957.* Viktor E. Frankl Collection, GTU 98-5-012, Graduate Theological Union Archives, Flora Lawson Hewitt Library, Graduate Theological Union, Berkeley CA. Audiotape.

———. *Viktor Frankl Recollections: An Autobiography.* New York: Plenum Press, 1997.

———. *The Will to Meaning.* New York: Meridian, 1988.

Frattaroli, Elio. *Healing the Soul in the Age of the Brain: Becoming Conscious in an Unconscious World.* New York: Viking, 2001.

Fromm, Erich. "The Limitations and Dangers of Psychology." In *Religion and Culture: Essays in Honor of Paul Tillich.* Edited by Walter Leibrecht (New York: Harper & Brothers, 1959) 36.

Fromm, Erich. *Psychoanalysis and Religion.* New Haven CT: Yale University Press, 1978.

Furedi, Frank. *Therapy Culture: Cultivating Vulnerability in an Uncertain Age.* London: Routledge, 2004.

Gardner, Howard. "Good Work: Where Excellence and Ethics Meet." *International Journal of Existential Psychology and Psychotherapy* 1/1 (July 2004): 16–27.

Gergen, Kenneth J. *An Invitation to Social Constructionism.* London: Sage Publications, 1999.

———. *Realities and Relationships: Soundings in Social Constructionism.* Cambridge MA: Harvard University Press, 1997.

———. *The Saturated Self: Dilemmas of Identity in Contemporary Life.* New York: Basic Books, 2000.

Gergen, Kenneth J. and Sheila McNamee. *Relational Responsibility: Resources for Suitable Dialogue.* Thousand Oaks CA: Sage Publishing, 1999.

Gill, Ajaipal Singh. *Frankl's Logotherapy and the Struggle Within.* Pittsburgh PA: Dorrance Publishing, 2000.

Gill, Robin. *Health Care and Christian Ethics.* Cambridge: Cambridge University Press, 2006.

Griffith, James L. and Melissa Elliott Griffith. *Encountering the Sacred in Psychotherapy: How to Talk With People About Their Spiritual Lives.* New York: Guilford Press, 2003.

Grollman, Earl A. "Viktor E. Frankl: A Bridge between Psychiatry and Religion." *Conservative Judaism* 14/1 (Fall 1964).

Healing: Human and Divine. Edited by Simon Doniger. New York: Association Press, 1957.

Helminiak, Daniel A. *Religion and the Human Sciences: An Approach Via Spirituality.* Albany NY: State University of New York Press, 1998.

Hiltner, Seward. *The Psychological Understanding of Religion.* Chester PA: Crozer Theological Seminary, 1947.

———. *Religion and Health.* New York: Macmillan Company, 1943.

———. *Self-Understanding Through Psychology and Religion.* New York: Charles Scribner's Sons, 1951.

Hoffding, Harald. *The Philosophy of Religion.* London: Macmillan and Co. Limited, 1931.

Hofmann, Hans. *Discovering Freedom.* Boston: Beacon Press, 1969.

———. "Immortality or Life." *Theology Today* 15/2 (July 1958): 1–12.

———. "Religion and Mental Health." *Journal of Religion and Health* 1/4 (July 1962): 319–36.

———. *Religion and Mental Health: A Casebook with Commentary and an Essay on Pertinent Literature.* New York: Harper & Brothers, 1961.

Homrighausen, E. G. "The Church in the World Today: To Make the Ministry Relevant." *Theology Today* 15/1 (April 1958): 1–6.

The Human Quest for Meaning. Edited by Paul T. P. Wong and Prem S. Fry. Mahwah NJ: Lawrence Erlbaum Associates, 1998.

Jones, James W. *In the Middle of This Road We Call Our Life.* New York: HarperSanFrancisco, 1995.

———. *Terror and Transformation: The Ambiguity of Religion in Psychoanalytic Perspective.* New York: Taylor and Francis, 2002.

Klingberg, Haddon, Jr. *When Life Calls Out to Us.* New York: Doubleday, 2001.

Koenig, Harold G. *Is Religion Good For Your Health: The Effects of Religion on Physical and Mental Health.* Binghamton NY: Haworth Press, 1997.

Koenig, Harold G. and Douglas M. Lawson. *Faith in the Future: Healthcare, Aging, and the Role of Religion.* Philadelphia: Templeton Foundation Press, 2004.

Kunz, George. *The Paradox of Power and Weakness: Levinas and an Alternative Paradigm for Psychology.* Albany NY: State University of New York Press, 1998.

———. "What Makes Therapy Therapeutic?" Address given at the orientation retreat for the graduate program in counseling psychology at Trinity Western University on 14 September 2002. www.meaning.ca/meaning_therapy/presentations/therapeutic_therapy.htm accessed 26 September 2004.

Längle, Alfried. "The Art of Involving the Person." *European Psychotherapy* 4/1 (2003): 47–58.

———. "Burnout—Existential Meaning and Possibilities of Prevention." *European Psychotherapy* 4/1 (2003): 129–44.

———. "Existential Analysis Psychotherapy." *The International Forum for Logotherapy* 13/1 (1990): 17–19.

———. "Goals and Motivations in Existential Psychotherapy: The Four Fundamental Conditions for a Fulfilled Existence." www.laengle.info/al/al_pu.li.php?sprache=en

———. "Objectives of Existential Psychology and Existential Psychotherapy: Answering Paul Wong's Editorial." *International Journal of Existential Psychology and Psychotherapy* 1/1 (July 2004): 99–102.

———. "Personal Existential Analysis." *Psychotherapies East and West: Integration of Psychotherapies* Korean Academy of Psychotherapists, Seoul Korea (1995): 348–64.

———. "The Search for Meaning in Life and the Existential Fundamental Motivations." *International Journal of Existential Psychology and Psychotherapy* 1/1 (July 2004): 28–37.

———. "Suffering: An Existential Challenge." Unpublished lecture presented in Warsaw, Poland, 22 March 2003. www.laengle.info/al/al_pu_li.php?sprache=en.

———. "What Are We Looking For When We Search for Meaning?" *Ultimate Reality and Meaning* 1/4 (Spring 1992): 306–14.

———. *Viktor Frankl: Ein Porträt.* Munich, Germany: PiperVerlag GmbH, 1998.

Längle, Alfried and Britt-Mari Sykes. "Viktor Frankl—Advocate for Humanity: On His 100th Birthday." *Journal of Humanistic Psychology* 6/1 (January 2006): 19–35.

Life Ethics in World Religions. Edited by Dawne C. McCance. Altanta: Scholars Press, 1998.

Lowenthal, Del and Robert Snell. *Post-Modernism for Psychotherapists: A Critical Reader.* New York: Brunner-Routledge, 2003.

Making the Ministry Relevant. Edited by Hans Hofmann. New York: Charles Scribner's Sons, 1960.

Martin Buber on Psychology and Psychotherapy: Essays, Letters and Dialogues. Edited by Judith Buber Agassi. Syracuse NY: Syracuse University Press, 1999.

May, Rollo. *The Discovery of Being.* New York: W. W. Norton & Company, 1983.

———. "Existential Psychiatry." *Journal of Religion and Health.* 1 (October 1961): 31–40.

———. *Man's Search for Himself.* New York: Delta, 1953.

———. *The Meaning of Anxiety.* New York: W. W. Norton & Company, 1977.

———. *Paulus: Tillich as Spiritual Leader.* Dallas: Saybrook, 1988.

McCann, Richard V. *The Churches and Mental Health.* New York: Basic Books, 1962.

Midgley, Mary. *Beast and Man: The Roots of Human Nature.* London: Routledge, 1998.

———. *The Ethical Primate: Humans, Freedom and Morality.* London: Routledge, 1994.

———. *The Myths We Live By.* London: Routledge, 2003.

———. *Science as Salvation: A Modern Myth and Its Meaning.* London: Routledge, 1996.

The Ministry and Mental Health. Edited by Hans Hofmann. New York: Association Press, 1960.

Mitchell, Kenneth R. "Paul Tillich's Contributions to Pastoral Psychology." *Pastoral Psychology* 19/181 (February 1968): 24–32.

Moskowitz, Eva S. *In Therapy We Trust: America's Obsession with Self-Fulfillment*. Baltimore MD: John Hopkins University Press, 2001.

The Nature of Man in Theological and Psychological Perspective. Edited by Simon Doniger. New York: Harper & Brothers, 1962.

New York Psychology Group of the National Council on Religion in Higher Education Papers. Minutes and papers from monthly meetings, 1941–1945. In possession of Dr. Allison Stokes, Ithaca College (Ithaca NY).

Oates, Wayne E. "The Contribution of Paul Tillich to Pastoral Psychology." *Pastoral Psychology* 19/181 (February 1968): 11–16.

One Hundred Years of Psychology and Religion: Issues and Trends in a Century Long Quest. Edited by Peter H. M. P. Roelofsma, Joseph M. T. Corveleyn, and Joke W. Van Saane. Amsterdam, Netherlands: VU University Press, 2003.

Parker, Ian. "Critical Psychology: Excitement and Danger." *The International Journal of Critical Psychology* 1/1 (2001): 127.

———. *Psychoanalytic Culture: Psychoanalytic Discourse in Western Society*. London: Sage Publications, 1997.

Paul Tillich in Conversation: Psychotherapy, Religion, Culture, History, Psychology. Edited by James B. Ashbrook. Bristol IN: Wyndham Hall Press, 1988.

Prilleltensky, Isaac. "Bridging Agency, Theory and Action: Critical Links in Critical Psychology." In *Critical Psychology: Voices for Change*. Edited by Tod Sloan. New York: St. Martin's Press, 2000.

———. "Emancipation, Epistemology, and Engagement: Challenges for Critical Psychology." In *The Journal for Critical Psychology*.).

———. *The Morals and Politics of Psychology: Psychological Discourse and the Status Quo*. Albany NY: State University of New York Press, 1994.

Prilleltensky, Issac and Geoffrey Nelson. *Doing Psychology Critically: Making a Difference in Diverse Settings*. New York: Palgrave Macmillan, 2002.

Psychiatry and Religious Experience. Edited by Louis Linn and Leo W. Schwarz. New York: Random House, 1958.

Psychohistory in Psychology of Religion: Interdisciplinary Studies. Edited by Jacob A. Belzen. Amsterdam, Netherlands: Editions Rodopi B.V., 2001.

Religion and Culture: Essays in Honor of Paul Tillich. Edited by Walter Leibrecht. New York: Harper & Brothers, 1959.

Religion and Health. Edited by Simon Doniger. New York: Association Press, 1958.

Religion and Psychology: Mapping the Terrain. Edited by Diane Jonte-Pace and William Parsons. New York: Routledge, 2001.

Richardson, Frank C., Blaine J. Fowers, and Charles B. Guignon. *Re-envisioning Psychology: Moral Dimensions of Theory and Practice.* San Francisco: Jossey-Bass, 1999.

Roberts, David E. *Psychotherapy and a Christian View of Man.* New York: Charles Scribner's Sons, 1950.

Robinson, Daniel N. *An Intellectual History of Psychology.* Madison WI: University of Wisconsin Press, 1981.

Rose, Nikolas. *Inventing Ourselves: Psychology, Power, and Personhood.* Cambridge: Cambridge University Press, 1998.

Rubin, Jeffrey. "Psychoanalysis is Self-Centered." In *Soul on the Couch: Spirituality, Religion and Morality in Contemporary Psychoanalysis.* Edited by Charles Spezzano and Gerald J. Gargiulo. Hillsdale NJ: Analytic Press, 1997.

Sartre, Jean-Paul. *Existential Psychoanalysis.* Washington D.C.: Regnery Publishing, 1981.

Schneider, Kirk J. *The Paradoxical Self: Toward an Understanding of Our Contradictory Nature.* Amherst NY: Humanity Books, 1999.

———. *Rediscovery of Awe: Splendor, Mystery, and the Fluid Center of Life.* St. Paul MN: Paragon House, 2004.

Schraube, Ernest. "Reflecting on Who We Are in a Technical World." In *Critical Psychology: Voices for Change.* Edited by Tod Sloan. New York: St. Martin's Press, 2000.

Schweiker, William. *Theological Ethics and Global Dynamics: In the Time of Many Worlds.* Malden MA; Oxford; and Victoria, Australia: Blackwell, 2004.

Science and the Search for Meaning. Edited by Jean Staune. Philadelphia: Templeton Foundation Press, 2006.

Simpson, Gary M. *Critical Social Theory: Prophetic Reason, Civil Society, and Christian Imagination.* Minneapolis MN: Fortress Press, 2002.

Singer, Peter. *Unsanctifying Human Life: Essays on Ethics.* Oxford & Malden MA: Blackwell, 2002.

Sloan, Tod. *Damaged Life: The Crisis of the Modern Psyche.* London and New York: Routledge, 1996.

———. *Life Choices: Understanding Dilemmas and Decisions.* Boulder CO: Westview Press, 1996.

Smail, David. *Illusion and Reality: The Meaning of Anxiety.* London: Constable and Company, 1997.

Sorenson, Randall Lehmann. *Minding Spirituality.* Hillsdale NJ: Analytic Press, 2004.

Spinelli, Ernesto. "Hell Is Other People: A Sartrean View of Conflict Resolution." *International Journal of Existential Psychology and Psychotherapy* 1/1 (July 2004): 56–65.

———. *The Mirror and the Hammer: Challenges to Therapeutic Orthodoxy.* London: Continuum, 2001.

———. *Tales of Un-Knowing: Eight Stories of Existential Therapy.* Washington Square: New York University Press, 1997.

Steinzor, Bernard. "Thinking Meaningfully About Emptiness." *Psychiatry and Social Science Review* 3/9 (September 1969): 26.

Stokes, Allison. *Ministry After Freud.* New York: Pilgrim Press, 1985.

Against the Third Reich: Paul Tillich's Wartime Radio Broadcasts into Nazi Germany. Edited by Ronald H. Stone and Matthew Lon Weaver. Louisville KY: Westminster John Knox Press, 1998.

Strenger, Mary Ann and Ronald H. Stone. *Dialogues of Paul Tillich.* Macon GA: Mercer University Press, 2002.

Sullivan, Edmund. *Critical Psychology and Pedagogy: Interpretation of the Personal World.* Toronto Canada: OISE Press, 1990.

Tillich, Hannah. *From Time to Time.* New York: Stein & Day, 1973.

Tillich, Paul. "The Concept of Faith in the Jewish Christian Tradition." Paper presented at the meeting of the New York Psychology Group. New York. 10 April 1942.

———. *The Courage to Be.* New Haven CT: Yale University Press, 1980.

———. *Dynamics of Faith.* New York: Harper Torchbooks, 1957.

———. *The Eternal Now.* New York: Charles Scribner's Sons, 1963.

———. "Existentialism and Psychotherapy." *Review of Existential Psychology and Psychiatry* 1 (1961): 8–16.

———. *The Future of Religions*. New York: Harper & Row, 1966.

———. *Love, Power and Justice*. London and New York: Oxford University Press, 1954.

———. *The Meaning of Health: Essays in Existentialism, Psychoanalysis, and Religion*. Edited by Perry LeFevre. Chicago: Exploration Press, 1984.

———. *My Travel Diary: 1936: Between Two Worlds*. New York and London: Harper & Row, 1970.

———. *The New Being*. New York: Charles Scribner's Sons, 1955.

———. *On the Boundary: An Autobiographical Sketch*. New York: Charles Scribner's Sons, 1966.

———. *The Religious Situation*. New York: Meridian Books, 1956.

———. *The Shaking of the Foundations*. New York: Charles Scribner's Sons, 1948.

———. *The Spiritual Situation in Our Technical Society*. Edited by J. Mark Thomas. Macon GA: Mercer University Press, 1988.

———. *Systematic Theology*. Volumes 1–3. Chicago: University of Chicago Press, 1967.

———. *Theology of Culture*. London and New York: Oxford University Press, 1959.

———. *Theology of Peace*. Louisville KY: Westminster/John Knox Press, 1990.

———. *The World Situation*. Philadelphia: Fortress Press, 1965.

Tolman, Charles W. *Psychology, Society, and Subjectivity: An Introduction to German Critical Psychology*. London and New York: Routledge, 1994.

Vanier, Jean. *Becoming Human*. Toronto, Canada: House of Anansi Press, 1998.

Viktor Frankl's Contribution to Spirituality and Aging. Edited by Melvin A. Kimble. New York: Haworth Pastoral Press, 2000.

Weiner, Bernard. "On Responsibility Inferences and the Perceived Moral Person." *International Journal of Existential Psychology and Psychotherapy* 1/1 (July 2004): 66–73.

Wong, Paul T. P. and Prem S. Fry. "Existential Psychology for the 21st Century." *International Journal of Existential Psychology and Psychotherapy* 1/1 (July 2004): 1–2.

Wulff, David. *Psychology of Religion: Classic and Contemporary Views.* New York: John Wiley and Sons, 1991.

Yalom, Irving. *Existential Psychotherapy.* New York: Basic Books, 1980.

———. *The Gift of Therapy: An Open Letter to a New Generation of Therapists and Their Patients.* New York: HarperCollins, 2002.

———. *Love's Executioner and Other Tales of Psychotherapy.* New York: Harper Perennial, 1989.

———. *Momma and the Meaning of Life: Tales of Psychotherapy.* New York: Basic Books, 1999.

Young, Robert M. "Postmodernism and the Subject: Pessimism of the Will." *Free Associations* 16 (1989): 81–96.

———. "The Search for Transcendent Values." http://www.shef.ac.uk/uni/academic/N-Q/psysc/staff/rmyoung/index.html. Accessed 15 October 2002.

The Viktor Frankl Audio & Video Library. Edited by Jeffrey K. Zeig. Phoenix AZ: Zeig, Tucker & Theisen. n.d.

Index

Adler, Alfred, 52
Allport, Gordon, 47, 66, 84
Anderson, Harlene, 114, 118
Appel, Kenneth, 83-84, 99
Auer, Edward, 99
Barbour, Ian, 145
Benedict, Ruth, 28
Bigham, Thomas, 20-21
Bone, Harry, 29, 31, 36-37, 40
Booth, Gotthard, 20-21, 84
Cali, Grace, 48
Cooper, Terry D., 12, 19
Doherty, William J., 104, 143
Elliott, Grace, 15, 32, 37-39
Emmons, Robert, 14, 105-106
Farris, Mutie Tillich, 15
Fowers, Blaine J., 112
Fox, Dennis, 110
Frankl, Viktor, 2-3, 17, 28, 34, 39, 43, 45-78, 81, 83, 87, 89, 93, 95-97, 100, 102, 113-119, 121, 125, 133, 142-143, 153-155
Frankley, Greta, 20
Fromm, Eric, 9, 17, 19-20, 26 -31, 34-36, 40, 64, 129, 130, 133
Furedi, Frank, 108
Gargiulo, Gerald, J. 111
Gergen, Kenneth J., 100
Glickman, Martha, 20, 33
Grollman, Earl A., 49, 51
Guignon, Charles B., 112
Hiltner, Seward, 5, 12, 17, 19-22, 26, 40, 83-84
Hofmann, Hans, 2-3, 7, 22, 47-48, 65, 79-86, 88-100, 126, 132, 155-156
Holzman, Lois, 109, 114
Homans, G.C., 84
Homrighausen, E.G., 84
Horney, Karen, 15
Jaspers. Karl, 127, 130, 153
Längle, Alfried, 17, 26, 35, 39, 41, 52, 91, 96-97, 127-128, 132, 134-140, 142, 144-145, 147-148, 150-152
Lefevre, Perry, 14
Leibrecht, Walter, 127
Leslie, Robert C., 66, 84
Lindemann, Eric, 84
Loomis, Earl A. Jr., 13, 84
Maiers, Wolfgang, 109
May, Rollo, 5-6, 13-14, 19-20, 30, 32
McCann, Richard, V., 27
Meserve, Harry C. Rev., 27
Midgley, Mary, 156
Morss, John, 109, 114
Moskowitz, Eva, 4, 101, 107
Nelson, Geoffrey, 110, 112
Niebuhr, Reinhold, 83-84
Owen Jane, 13
Parker, Ian, 112
Parsons, Talcott, 83
Pauck, Wilhelm and Marion, 12
Prilleltensky, Isaac, 110-112, 124-125
Rice, Otis, 21, 39-40
Richardson, Frank C., 112
Roberts, David, 18, 20, 24, 29-30, 38, 41 – 44, 154-155
Rogers, Carl, 20-21, 37, 41, 151
Rohrbach, Elizabeth, 29
Rubin, Jeffrey, 111, 113
Sasnett, Martene, 66
Sasnett, Randolph, 66
Schachtel, Ernest, 20
Schneider, Kirk, 14, 105
Schraube, Ernest, 113
Sloan, Tod, 110-111, 113
Sorensen, Randall Lehmann, 105

Spezzano, Charles, 111
Spinelli, Ernesto, 109, 111
Steinzor, Bernard, 49, 51
Stokes, Allison, 5, 12-13, 19-21, 81, 123, 145, 154
Stone, Ronald, 14, 120-121
Sullivan, Edmund, 108, 110-111
Thomas, J. Mark, 118
Tillich, Hannah, 15, 19
Tillich, Paul, 1-3, 10-15, 18, 21, 23, 31- 33, 37, 40-41, 43, 47-48, 83-84, 96-97, 100, 102, 113-126, 128-130, 143-153
Tolman, Charles W., 109
Weaver, Matthew Lon, 14, 120-121
Wickes, Francis G., 20
Wong, Paul, 130
Wulff, David, 103